PAST SHOCK

THE ORIGIN OF RELIGION AND ITS IMPACT ON THE HUMAN SOUL

Jack Barranger

The Prometheus Project

© 1998, 2001
Jack Barranger

This book was published for
The Prometheus Project
by The Book Tree.

For additional information and
a catalog of related titles contact:

The Prometheus Project
c/o Post Office Box 724
Escondido, California 92033

1 (800) 700-TREE

LAYOUT AND DESIGN BY:

Tédd St. Rain

COVER IMAGE: Adam and Eve being expelled from the Garden of Eden
after eating from the Tree of Knowledge.

TO LOKI
Who drove the gods from the earth

TO PROMETHEUS
Who stole fire from the gods

TO THE HUMAN RACE
Which is about to break free

TABLE OF CONTENTS

INTRODUCTION

One of the great challenges of all humankind is to bring clarity to the understanding of the human condition: who we are, why we are and where we are going. That is what Jack Barranger does so well in this important book.

At first glance, the average person might find his theories rather outlandish. True, they go far beyond what the mainstream would consider as acceptable, but I've found, over my own years of research, that the more you look into the puzzle of humanity, the more the theories within this book make sense.

Jack admits that he does not have all the answers, and is not claiming to have the ultimate truth but he backs up what he says with solid research. But we will never get any closer to the truth, without being bold enough to explore in the proper directions. This involves overriding some powerful programming we received in the past. This programming set us solidly into a frame of mind that is difficult to escape without immense efforts and insight.

We are the victims of genetic as well as psychological programming. Very few people have been able to unravel exactly how these forces were put into place and how they affect us today. With Past Shock comes many answers. Page after page brings new insights as pieces to humanity's puzzle fall into place. The book brings excitement as you turn each page since things begin to make sense regarding who and what mankind is, but at the same time you can be uncomfortable with its message because this is new and unknown territory for even the most seasoned researchers. Be prepared: reading *Past Shock* will bring you some present shock.

I was inspired to write this Introduction just after completing a recent book called *Triumph of the Human Spirit: The Greatest Achievements of the Human Soul and How Its Power Can Change Your Life*. It is about spiritual freedom fighters throughout history, how they attempted to break us free from this programming, and how we can break free ourselves. After months of personal research, I have found that reading *Past Shock* has added to my understanding of the root of our problems, what the people in my book were fighting for and why we must become spiritually free. Occasionally, someone comes along in history like Barranger who

7

8

wakes his readers up and notices who we are and what we can really be. In a collective sense, humanity is showing signs of awakening from a deep spiritual slumber. This book, *Past Shock*, has the potential to sound an alarm to a sleeping humanity. Being exposed to it ideas will speed up this wake up call. I urge you to partake of its wisdom.

Barranger's claims that ancient religion may be impacting humanity today is not an attempt at irreverence or blasphemy. He makes it very clear that the blasphemy was committed by the gods of our ancient past. They created humans as a slave race. They trained humans to fight their wars. Finally, they created religion as a means of conditioning and manipulation. Barranger refers to these gods as the "pretender gods" because they demanded being worshipped when they were not worthy of being worshipped. He makes it very clear that the conditioning of these gods lingers on today and impacts our modern religious beliefs — and our view of ourselves.

What impresses me the most is the clarity of this book. Barranger does not mince words or get into long diatribes. He tells things like they are based on historical texts, his own personal experience and a logical synthesis based on eighteen years of research. (He teaches Research and Critical Thinking at the college level). Much of our religious dogma in today's world is not based on clear thinking. It's based more on blind faith instead of logic, reason, or common sense. You will come away from this book with incredibly clear ideas – revolutionary ideas – but ones that make perfect sense. Chances are, you have never thought about Adam and Eve, human creation, the Great Flood and God Himself in the ways portrayed in this book. The ideas herein may upset many people because old ideas die hard. What *Past Shock* will do is cause you to look at some of those old ideas in a totally different light.

Sadly, comfort zones are considered more sacred than the truth that lies outside of them. This is not a book for people who want to remain in well established comfort zones. If, however, you welcome new ideas, chances are you will find yourself surprised with the information and thinking in new ways about yourself and your place in the universe. I can assure you that what you'll find in this powerful book is nothing short of groundbreaking information.

Rev. Paul Tice
November 1998

A WORD TO THE READER

In the two years I have spent researching and writing this book, much has happened regarding what people believe about their origins. Thanks to shows like *The X Files* and material on The Learning Channel and The Discovery Channel, the idea that life alien to our own is much more commonly explored and accepted.

This is not yet another book on UFOs. Our bookstores are polluted with hundreds of titles attempting to explain what UFOs are, why millions of people are claiming to be abducted by aliens, and what this might mean for the future. If I were concerned about the future, I would have titled this book *Future Shock* and thus faced a lawsuit from the publishers of Alvin Toffler's effective study. His book explains how the future is so quickly encroaching upon people that they are in a state of "future shock."

Thus, this book is not about UFOs in the present. However, it touches very strongly on the possibility that inhabitants of UFOs in our past treated humans so badly that we still have not recovered from their impact. I refer to this lingering impact as "past shock."

While writers like Zecharia Sitchin, Neil Freer, Lloyd Pye, Alan Alford, Erik von Daniken and R.A. Boulay have explored the theme of gods from our past impacting humanity, most books dealing with this highly controversial subject have focused mainly on history. *Past Shock* will refer to this history but it will also focus more on the psychological impact that these extraterrestrials made upon humanity. This impact lingers on today, and it is not serving us well.

In one of the most tragic of ironies, the majority of humans continue to worship those "gods" who abused them the most. This shows up in our highly outdated propensity to do battle and our church's ability to manipulate people's belief systems. The need to worship an anthropomorphic God is the result of "past shock." The abuses that continue in the name of God and religion are the result of "past shock." Our seeming ease in using wars as a solution to problems (or a "blooding" to prove manhood) is influenced by "past shock." Our belief that the often-incomprehensible Bible is the word of God stems more from "past shock" than divine inspiration. Our belief that Yahweh/Jehovah could be the God of the Universe shows how well "past shock" can still condition humanity today.

9

This book will explore the crimes of gods like Yahweh [Jehovah], Enlil, Nannar-Sin, and other god figures from thousands of years ago. These pages will reveal traits of these gods which are anything but godly.

A Working Hypothesis

However, unlike those who insist that their particular set of scriptures are the divine inspired word of God, this book will not be as dogmatic. Dogma dilutes exploration. Instead I present this work as a working hypothesis. I believe that there is good evidence that extraterrestrials (or highly advanced beings from this planet) created humans as a slave force to do heavy labor. Documents, including the Old Testament provide very good evidence that humans were eventually trained to fight wars for their gods. Eventually, the gods created religion as a means to keep the increasing hordes of humans in line. In the ultimate act of "spiritual terrorism," these gods created a flood that destroyed most of the human species.

That certainly must have been a shock. If God created this flood, what does this say about God?

This book will explore the working hypothesis that it was not God who brought about the flood, but instead a group of pretenders who claimed that they were God. This heinous act has done more collective harm to the human psyche than any act in human history. This is the very core of past shock, and its fallout continues with great power today.

This is admittedly very controversial material. What will make this exploration upsetting to some is that a plethora of documents from thousands of years ago exists to point out the horrors that were inflicted upon the emerging human race. Much of the material used in *Past Shock* comes from the *Old Testament.* However, what is revealed here does not show up in Bible studies or sermons. This is powerful material.

Why not just claim that I have stumbled upon the truth? Because that is a trait of past shock: the need to be told what the truth is – without any need or even permission to explore for oneself. Past shock rears its ugly head when people embrace the faith of their parents without any exploration on their own. Be warned: you are about to embark on an exploration that could significantly change your life.

However, this exploration is a working hypothesis.

What exactly is a working hypothesis?

Any researcher or explorer uses a working hypothesis when he is not completely sure of the truth of the material he is studying. The great psychologist Abraham Maslow used a working hypothesis when he advanced his theory of peak experiences. In his studies he discovered that humans had moments in which they experienced life so fully that their level of consciousness was at a peak. Some had two or three of these experiences in a lifetime. Others had these experiences two or three times a week.

For years, Maslow observed and researched his working hypothesis until he had enough evidence to prove that peak experiences were indeed a part of the human experience.

At present, the theory of black holes remains in the realm of working hypothesis. One has not yet seen or definitely been able to prove that such a thing as black holes exist. Yet the dogmatism of modern science insists that they have enough evidence to prove that black holes exist.

We don't yet have enough evidence, and the theory of black holes may still come crashing down once more evidence is gathered. We actually have about 100 times the evidence that UFOs are a reality, but science doesn't even want to deal with this material – perhaps because it is too close to home.

Another scientific working hypothesis that appears to be heading for the rock pile is the big bang theory. In our institutions of higher learning, this working hypothesis has been peddled off as truth. It most likely isn't. Evidence is surfacing which could possibly disprove the big bang theory. The fact that this was presented as the truth says more about the state of modern science than it does about how the universe was created.

Past Shock will do its best to avoid the arrogance that has plagued the scientific community. As *Past Shock's* author, I am aware that I am still in the realm of working hypothesis with the theories this book will explore. However, like Maslow's exploration of peak experiences, my fifteen years of research into this area leads me to believe that the ideas presented in this book are much closer to the truth about what happened thousands of years ago than most history and religious books convey.

We Have Been Misled

I strongly believe that we have been conned. We have been led to believe that the entity that the *Old Testament* describes as a mass murderer and heinous leader is the God of the Universe. Emerging evidence points to a much different reality.

We have been led to think that the slaughter of human beings in the name of God is a divine act. This is more closely related to what newly created humans were conditioned to believe thousands of years ago. And in the name of past shock, that conditioning plagues us today. For many, it is very difficult to overcome.

We have been led to believe that religions were something that resulted from a loving God to keep humans on the straight and narrow. This book will explore the extremely controversial hypothesis that religions were created to insure that humans would never experience the true God.

We have been led to believe that the creation of humans was an act of love. This book will use the *Old Testament* and other ancient texts to advance the theory that humans were created to be slaves, to do the menial works that the gods had become tired of doing. Toward the end of *Past Shock*, we will explore how our present attitudes toward life – and the slave chip mentality which we live it by – is the result of how our creators conditioned us thousands of years ago.

The above ideas are part of my working hypothesis. My research leads me to believe that we have not been told the truth about our ancient past. Join me on a journey of exploration into what might have really happened thousands of years ago.

If we have been conditioned by gods who are no longer with us, this discovery alone is the beginning of a new personal freedom.

If I come to a dead end with my working hypothesis, then we are left with having to find other reasons for why we continue to condition ourselves in the name of God. We will continue to believe in a limited view of God rather than experiencing the true God, believing in the religion we grew up with rather than exploring religion with an open mind, and accepting what we are told about the "word of God" rather than researching this for ourselves. Read on and draw your own conclusions. However, realize that in this exploration, you are going to have to be very brave.

CHAPTER ONE

The Past – Through a Glass Darkly

For some, this will be a very upsetting book. Claiming that this book's main thesis is controversial is like claiming 1945's Hiroshima blast created some warmth. I would like nothing better than to be wrong about most everything I write here.

How wonderful it would be if God were in His heaven and all were right with the world. However, "God" (as "He" is seen by many of the main religions today) raped free will and refused to follow the Star Trek prime directive of not interfering with an emerging species. Ironically, He did not intervene during the Holocaust when "His" alleged chosen people were being murdered by the millions. "He" did not tear the place apart and overturn tables during the Spanish Inquisition. "He" did not save any innocent people from being burned as witches. When "God" does appear to intervene, it is during an eighteen-car crash when "He" saves only a select few. This "God" is so petty that – in some religious circles – daring to think that he doesn't exist or that he might be a total jerk for not intervening during crises could get you a one-way ticket to hell. What we have is the paradox of a God who intervened in history thousands of years ago but now – when "He" is most needed – is strangely absent.

Some may think that I am sarcastic – or even bitter – about God. I'm not. I am a theologically trained college teacher who – based on many years of research – believes that the true God is the victim of a "bad press." This bad press comes from what some very influential people insist are sacred books: The *Old Testament*, The *New Testament*, The *Bhagavad Gita*, The *Atra Hasis*, the *Mahabharata*, the *Popul Vuh*, and others.

The *Old Testament* portrays God as an entity, who by his own admission, is a jealous God and that he intends to wreak vengeance. The Sumerian *Atra Hasis* portrays "the gods" as the creators of humans. However, in this sacred book, humans are created as a hybrid race mainly for the purpose of doing slave labor. The Mayan sacred book, the *Popul Vuh*, portrays God as being so petty that he needs six creations to get humans

13

so fine-tuned that they are dumbed down from their original brilliance. After some "back to the drawing boards" anguish and five tries later, the clear seeing, highly independent human creations finally become compliant enough to worship their creators and take orders without protest.

Consensus Reality Gone Awry

This misguided consensus reality claims that the *Old Testament* is the truth (history) and that the *Atra Hasis* and the *Popul Vuh* are mythological creations. How interesting that even the most conservative of theologians now accept that the early chapters of the book of "Genesis" were taken directly from the Sumerian *Atra Hasis* (which was written more than a thousand years before the *Old Testament*).

Why was I compelled to write this book? The truth is crying out to be heard, and the record needs to be set straight. The truth about those who pretended to be God desperately needs to be explored. (Those who pretended to be God will be referred to in this book as the pretender gods.) Am I suggesting that Jehovah wasn't God? I am not only suggesting it, but I am also actually stating it as a historical reality and a present truth.

While it is easy for most people to believe that Zeus wasn't God, most of those same people will gasp with shock at the mere suggestion that Jehovah (Yahweh) wasn't God. The fact that Jehovah told his creations that he was God doesn't make it true. The Sumerian god Enlil told his creations that he was God, and he wasn't. Zeus roared that he was chief of all gods – and he wasn't. Jehovah insisted to followers who didn't know any better that he was the true God.

Yet he wasn't. He was like Zeus and Enlil: a stentorian pretender god.

The fact that all of Jehovah's pronouncements are couched within the aura of "sacred scripture" does not in any way move Jehovah any higher than simply being what he was – a pretender to the throne of the true God. Jehovah was nothing more than a highly egotistical, pompous warlord who had a lot to gain by lying about his true identity. By telling an emerging human race that he was the true God, he was able to manipulate the emerging humans into following and worshipping rather than creating and spiritually evolving.

Anyone free of Sunday school conditioning and religious indoctrination can sense this with just a little bit of research and exploration. The seven books of Zecharia Sitchin's *Earth Chronicles* series present solid evidence that the *Old Testament* and the *Bhagavad Gita* are not the only significant sacred documents to come from our ancient past. Sitchin is an explorer worthy of being compared to those who traced the source of the Nile or those who finally reached both Poles. One of the rare scholars fluent in both ancient Hebrew and the ancient Sumerian language, Zecharia

Sitchin has blazed trails to a deeper understanding of what really happened in humanity's ancient history. The discoveries of ancient Sumerian and Assyrian manuscripts along with the discovery of the Dead Sea Scrolls (1947) and the Nag Hamadi library (1945) will challenge past views of history and move humanity closer to the truth about what really happened in our ancient past.

It was an ugly time. Not even the *Old Testament* can disguise the horrors of those times. The earth was in violent turmoil following the catastrophic flood. Vivid accounts of plagues, earthquakes, volcanoes, and other acts of nature accompanied the Israelites' exodus. However, a further exploration of the *Old Testament* account points out that the real horror in this turbulent period may have been the pretender gods who conducted a spiritual reign of terror upon helpless humans.

Read some of the Bible's more violent stories to a child without using the names Jehovah, Yahweh, or God, and any child will quickly sense that "God" is anything but heroic. In fact, Jehovah – absent from conditioning and indoctrination – would be classified as a borderline psychotic.

As long as Jehovah is seen as God, the true God languishes in the darkness, impotent to help a human race stuck on worshipping the ancient pretender gods. The purpose of this book is to expose those pretenders. An equally important purpose is to point a light into this darkness and reveal where humanity very understandably and helplessly went astray. Humanity never fell by its own choice; instead, humanity was collectively shoved into a pit of ignorance by pretender gods who had much to gain by keeping these humans in the dark.

Another purpose of this book is to point out what impact these pretender gods had on the human experience. In the late 1960s author Alvin Toffler wrote *Future Shock*, pointing out how the quickly changing world around us was putting humanity into a state of shock. Toffler brilliantly pointed out how having a rapidly increasing number of choices created "overchoice" – a condition of helplessness stemming from the mind's increasing inability to process an increasing number of choices. *Future Shock* was, and still is, a brilliant book.

The Beginning of Past Shock

However, humanity has a much greater problem than future shock. Humanity was treated so brutally by these pretender gods that people today are still reeling from this past impact. Yet, most of humanity is in collective denial about this. The records in all sacred scriptures – if read free of conditioning and indoctrination – point to a spiritual rape of humanity's collective mind and soul.

In "future shock," the main problem is having too many choices.

With "past shock," humanity had too few choices.

These newly emerging humans were treated very badly, especially when they dared to suggest that they should have more choices. Later chapters will point out how dreadfully few choices humanity had. Even the pretender gods' creation of religion eventually caused humans to "voluntarily" limit their choices even further.

By insisting that many of the sacred scriptures are mythology, we collectively keep our heads firmly entrenched in the sands of spiritually correct ignorance. The majority of people continue to embrace 5,000 years of collective denial. Most continue believing that a perverse warlord who mentally, emotionally, and spiritually abused his people was God. Most close their minds to the simple idea that a loving God would never train his chosen people to slaughter innocent people. This began when the Israelites descended upon the people of Canaan and slaughtered them despite the fact that they had never provoked the Israelites.

In modern times, few have the courage to ask "Did Joshua have just cause for his slaughter of the people of Jericho?" After that horrendous slaughter, we encounter another inhumane event which most Biblical scholars close our minds to. One man named Achan was brutally stoned to death simply because he kept a wedge of gold and some silver for himself. This occurred after he participated in the slaughter of Jericho's men, women, and children.

The logic here is quite perverse. Evidently it was okay to slaughter innocent men, women, and children. However, keeping some of the booty for oneself was a sin requiring severe punishment far in excess of the crime.

Few dare to suggest that this is one pretender god that sorely needed to have his posterior firmly kicked. However, in the times of past shock, no force was powerful enough to do the kicking.

Most collectively block out the absurdity of Jehovah striking Uzzah dead simply because he saw that the Ark of the Covenant was going to crash to the ground and tried to save it. He moved quickly to save the precious relic, and by the biblical account, Jehovah struck him dead.

This was indeed Jehovah – but not God.

These events – as well as others mentioned in the Bible and other sacred scriptures – point out a time in history when it was terrifying to be a member of the human race. Entities with a greater technology, greater mind power, and a greater physical strength brutally mistreated their newly created humans. They conditioned and humiliated their new creations to fight wars for them much in the same manner that British colonialists got their "savage blacks" to fight for England in nineteenth century Africa.

This jolted us, for we were a relatively new species. When we eventually started to rebel, these pretender gods created the eventual means of manipulation – a religion which promised eternal rest if only one continued working as a slave in Earth time. Another proviso was thrown in to make the manipulation totally effective and complete. Deviate from this religion and you will not only be in misery during your lifetime on Earth – you will be in misery for eternity. The fact that people still believe this today points out how effectively the conditioning of the past strangles many today.

Humanity is still collectively reeling from what was done thousands of years ago. The healing cannot be fully completed until we discover [1] why we were created, [2] what happened to us after we were created, and [3] how religion was established to insure that we remained true to those who dared to claim that they were God.

I have been a religious person most of my life. It was only as I was approaching my forties that I began to understand the harm which religion might have done thousands of years ago – and the harm that much of it creates today. I trained to be a fundamentalist minister who would preach the "good news." How easy that would have been in twentieth century America. However, as I read much of the Bible in its original language and researched more deeply into mythology, I realized that I would be doing a greater service to humanity if I "screwed my courage to the sticking place" and began telling people the bad news we've been ignoring.

Bad News for Ancient Man

The bad news is that humanity is a species still reeling from the past shock. This condition was perpetuated by a group of technologically advanced entities that had the gall to tell us that they were God. They were only pretending, but we didn't know that! We didn't have the powers of perception that we have now.

Whether these entities were highly advanced beings, survivors from Atlantis, technologically superior humans from a parallel universe, extra-dimensional beings, or extraterrestrials is not an issue at this point in the book. Many good books effectively support each possibility. What we will explore is the fact that they were pretenders to godhood, and they created religion as a means to prevent our spiritual development.

The good news is that once humanity begins to discover what really happened in the past, it can begin getting free of this horrifying past and experience greater levels of spiritual and personal freedom.

The bad news is that the truth hurts. What happened in our past is so ugly that the understandable human response is to block it out.

Relating to this, some other good news is that if we bravely face the past with all its ugliness, we can move forward with a greater potential for humanity.

Many humans are very effectively conditioned. Some would rather continue the spiritual rape than break free of its fallout. Others would insist that my thesis smacks of secular humanism. This is too often a term used by some conservative Christians to stifle free thought. Put a nasty label on it, and it will go away. Others continue to believe that any attempt to liberate ourselves from spiritual slavery would not be pleasing to Almighty God.

Spiritual liberation and embracing our human potential was immensely offensive to Jehovah and his ilk. It would have been grossly offensive to the Sumerian god Enlil who set into motion the creation of humans to be slaves. Enlil and the other gods saw no other role for humans other than to serve. Such attempts to liberate humans would have also been intensely offensive to Zeus. One need only see what Zeus did to Prometheus when Prometheus stole fire from the gods and gave it to humanity. Prometheus was chained to a rock where vultures pecked at his exposed liver. Greek myth informs us that this happened for a very long time until Zeus finally decided to free Prometheus.

However, a terrifying archetype looms here. Participate in the liberation of humans, and you're in deep trouble.

Certainly the horrors of the Garden of Eden should be ample proof of

PROMETHEUS STOLE FIRE FROM THE GODS AND GAVE IT TO HUMANITY.

the pettiness of Jehovah. Eating of the fruit increased knowledge (gnosis) and caused Adam and Eve to see more clearly. This is what the serpent wanted for Adam and Eve: clarity of vision and a greater human potential. However, Jehovah went into ungodly rage and reacted with savage retaliation: kicking both out of the garden of Eden, ensuring that all men would have to work hard for their food, and promising that all women would suffer pain in childbirth.

That is the horror of past shock. Humans still believe that God wants them to be hymn singing, highly indoctrinated slaves who continue to use only a small portion of their brains. The horror of past shock is that we still limit ourselves in the name of piety and spirituality. We wrongly believe that God would be angry if we dared to develop to our full potential as humans.

The Conditioning Lingers On

Because of past shock, humanity collectively walks this planet as slaves. Because of past shock, too many still fear an angry God rather than becoming still and listening to the whisperings of the true God. Because of past shock, some factions of the religious experience condemn meditation, dream analysis, the development of psychic senses because that past conditioning says, "Ye are slaves and so shalt ye remain as slaves."

How different that is from Jesus' pronouncement of "Ye are gods."

How ironic that the Rabbi Jesus could state "You shall know the truth, and the truth shall set you free," yet what is presented today as that truth are lies which insult the truth of the true God. Because of past shock, too many still reel at the fear of hell. Many look for cheap and quick levels of fire insurance to assure a good life in the great beyond. By focusing on the next life, too many lose the capacity to live abundantly in this life. The creation of religion in our ancient past keeps many presently indoctrinated to the idea that the "next life" is more important than this one.

Because of past shock most of humanity still walks in darkness, still worships a dark god, and still lead lives of quiet desperation. As mentioned before, this book's working hypothesis is that thousands of years ago humans were psycho-spiritually raped by pretender gods who first created humans and then exploited them. Eventually, religion entered the picture as a form of deeper manipulation. This fear-motivation kept the human slaves working instead of rebelling. With both a promise of eternal rest and the fear of an everlasting hell, the near helpless human race was paradoxically conditioned to experience a "hell" on earth so that its people would escape hell in the eternal life which would follow.

This is one of the most brutal ironies in human history.

All of this conditioning was a dastardly deed. Yet it worked. Its fallout lingers today as humanity collectively struggles under the massive weight of the pretender gods' awesome conditioning. Our ancient past was a very dark time. Within us, the darkness lingers on.

This book's exploration will shine a light into the darkness. I do not see myself as a liberator or guru. I do see myself as one who wants to share what I have learned from years of painstaking research. I am not attached to being completely right. In fact, new discoveries will eventually prove me wrong in some areas. These new discoveries will also bring another irony: the fact that I may not have been bold enough in some of my explorations.

CHAPTER TWO

History's Lowest Moment:
The Beginnings of Past Shock

Long ago something happened – something so painful that few possess the courage to look at it. Thousands of years ago a group of beings raped our souls. That not being horrible enough, this group of "advanced" beings claimed that this soul rape was good for us – that what they were doing was in our best interests. And they created religion as a means to insure that once they were gone, we could continue to condition ourselves in ways that would insure that our slavery would continue.

These beings claimed that they were God, and then they perpetuated upon us some of the most ungodly acts in human history. These so-called "advanced beings" used us. When we became useless, they discarded us. While they spoke of saving our souls, their actions reflected acts that contributed more to destroying our souls.

In that ancient of days, we were newly formed, immensely naive, and dangerously trusting. These "advanced beings" told us that they were our creators. Increasing evidence shows that, at least to some degree, this might indeed be true. They also told us that we would be rewarded if we obeyed them and did exactly what they told us to do. In this area they were deceitful. They rewarded us only when it served their needs. From their "godly" perspective we were created by them to be exploited by them, to serve them, and eventually to worship them.

We were their slaves, and they were masters at convincing us that being their slaves was all for the glory of God.

And we bought it.

We are still buying it, despite the fact that these "advanced beings" have long since departed.

In The *Epic of Gilgamesh* and the Sumerian epic the *Atra Hasis,* these beings were known as the Anunnaki. In the *Book of Enoch,* these beings were known as The Shining Ones. The ancient Greeks right up to the time of The Golden Age of Greece simply referred to them as "the gods."

The sacred scriptures of the ancient Hebrews referred to them as the Elohim, the Nefilim, and the Raiphiam/Rephaim.

When Past Shock Began

More than 2,800 years ago, they were here. Shortly after 800 B.C.E. these gods left their human creations to fend for themselves. Their leaving eliminated the cause and catalyst for the insanity. However, their leaving did not stop the insanity. Reeling from their egregious past shock, we now have a massive Stockholm Syndrome. This is the condition which causes people to side with their captors, as Patty Hearst did when she was captured and brutally treated by the Symbionese Liberation Army. She eventually embraced her captors' beliefs and helped them rob a bank.

As Patty Hearst had loyally embraced those who tortured her and continually locked her in a dark closet, so did the emerging human race loyally embrace the departed creator gods who had raped their souls and taken advantage of their trust and innocence.

Today, most of humanity still has its collective heads stuck firmly in the sand. Most still believe that these low creatures could be the true God. However, we have evolved into a strange breed of ostrich. Somehow we have been able to convince ourselves that Poseidon, Zeus, and Athena are the result of a highly creative people's imagination. We do the same with the lesser-known Sumerian gods Enki, Enlil, and Ninhursag. However, go a few hundred miles southeast or southwest and Jehovah (Yahweh) is not simply a real life entity. He is God. At least that is where consensus reality stands as humanity approaches the next millennium.

Somehow, this entity provided ten commandments which he himself never honored. This entity threatened his own created people with extermination. He turned his back on the people he claimed to have chosen as his own. Yet he is still seen as God, no matter how ungodly his acts or heinous his crimes. Jehovah (Yahweh) was simply one of a bevy of beings who did not have humanity's welfare as a high priority.

Actually, these beings not only raped our souls and violated our spiritual sovereignty but they also totally twisted the way we would view the true God. Thanks to their "divine invasion" we were conditioned to think of God as an angry warrior, one needing territory and food in order to keep him happy. These "gods" helped us to see ourselves as sinful and incomplete. They even managed to convince us that there was something holy about this incompleteness.

They lied to us by telling us that they were God. This is not recorded in obscure fragments of mythology. Instead, their egotistical pronouncements can be found in the *Old Testament*, the *Mahabharata*, The *Atra*

Hasis, and the *Bhagavad Gita*. Most people read the Bible and see Jehovah as God. (After all, didn't he tell us that he was?) Those who have gotten caught up in the Far Eastern religious fad see Krishna as a spiritual leader – one of the Hindu gods.

However, most of the people who insist on this view have not read deeply into the *Mahabharata* and the *Bhagavad Gita*. For some reason people exploring these two "holy books" fail to see that Krishna was a warmonger who goaded a peace-loving Arjuna into fighting a bloody war. The fact that a majority of people still believe that something holy exists in the ancient Israelites slaughter of hundreds of thousands of people and the fact that Arjuna was eventually harassed into fighting, point out how effective the pretender gods' conditioning was... and still is.

Modern Fallout from Ancient Past Shock

Thanks to the staying power of this conditioning, the Bosnian Serbs and the Bosnian Muslims continue to slaughter each other. The fact that many of these people might have been lifetime friends or neighbors is irrelevant. Conditioning – particularly ancient, archetypal conditioning – tragically transcends friendship and human values. This allegedly has stopped because thousands of U.N. troops are stationed in Bosnia. How ironic: thousands of soldiers are needed to stop people who think they are on a divine mission from God from killing each other.

Thanks to the staying power of this ancient conditioning, Rwandans slaughtered each other to the count of more than a million people. (Hutus slaughtered Tutsis, and Tutsis slaughtered Hutus. The fact that these two tribes had coexisted for years side-by-side suddenly became irrelevant.) Journalists claimed that four thousand dead bodies a week flowed down Rwanda's largest river.

What was it that lay deep in everyone's ancient archetypes[1] that allowed such a slaughter?

What shocks from the past could have had such driving power that the Rwandan slaughter was done with such ease and efficiency?

Thanks to this ancient conditioning Hitler exterminated as many as six million Jews in such a manner that not even the people being exterminated offered significant resistance. Could some shock have occurred in

---

[1] An archetype is a concept invented by the Swiss psychologist Carl Gustav Jung. Jung claimed that certain aspects of our ancient past lay deeply embedded in our unconscious minds. In fact, Jung went a step further and claimed that these archetypes were in the collective unconscious minds of people. Our obsession with heroes, our urge to protect our families and our urge to hunt animals all stem from archetypes established in humanity's ancient history. According to Jung, our need to fight wars, our need to experience an anthropomorphic higher being, and our tendency to want to return to paradise are also collective archetypes which impact us.

the past which so numbed the mid-twentieth century Germans that walking 600 people a day through death camps like Sobibor became as simple as driving home from work? Could something so shocking have happened in the past that such heinous actions were merely a repeat of ancient programming?

Perhaps death comes so easily now, because it came so easily thousands of years ago.

One thousand ships did sail to Troy to recover one kidnapped woman. We finally have moved this event from mythology to ancient history. Anyone who has read the *Iliad* knows the graphic descriptions of speared men with entrails hanging outside of them. Even the death of the men's horses is portrayed in chilling details. Achilles' final slaughter of Hector is both brutal and graphic. Yet Achilles' glee and righteousness in dragging the dead body of Hector around the outskirts of Troy requires a certain brutality which centers more on conditioning than Achilles' temporary wrath.

Yes, Hector had killed Patrocolos, Achilles' closest friend. Yet during the lulls in that ten-year war, Achilles and Hector were friends. Some apocryphal accounts tell of Achilles playing with Hector's children. Achilles had meaningful conversations with Hector's wife, Andromache. Yet something very deep took over when Achilles, in a fit of rage, not only killed Hector in hand to hand combat but also dragged his dead body around the walls of Troy in a state of egomaniacal rage. (Doesn't this have a familiar ring when one hears tales of once-friendly neighbors in Bosnia, and other parts of the world, killing each other?)

The final loss of wrath occurs when Achilles surrenders Hector's mutilated body to Hector's father, King Priam. This is one of the most moving scenes in world literature. Achilles reveals a compassion that breaks through ancient conditioning and allows more humane values to emerge.

Sadly, humane values such as these too often were overcome by a more powerful conditioning. This devastating ancient conditioning was instilled into humans long ago. Beings who were technologically and psychologically superior conditioned us to "fight for God." If we did not fight – or dared to run in the heat of battle – punishment lay waiting which was worse than being gutted or killed in that battle.

This conditioned us well: "Conscience doth make warriors of us all."

This conditioning was so effective that we eventually believed it was noble to fight battles for a group of heinous "gods" who were too lazy to fight their own battles.

Our Conditioned Need to Obey and Fight

If Jehovah said "Go and slay the Philistines," we went – glad to fight for God. During the Second World War both the Germans and the Americans thought they were allegedly fighting on God's side. You will find this is most any war throughout history.

One of history's most egregious and savage moments was the Crusades. In the name of Christ, Christians raped the women of the men they had just killed and then roasted babies, eating their seared flesh. When especially hungry for blood, some members of the Crusades attacked and slaughtered their fellow Christians on their journey home.

What else could they do? They had run out of Arabs to kill. And oh how it must have hurt to have that wily Arab leader Saladin actually prevent the Christians from "taking Jerusalem from the infidel" and restoring that city to Christendom. They must have been fit to be tied.

Actually, the Crusaders were very well conditioned. The conditioning had actually begun thousands of years before. In so many ways, the horror of the Crusades was a rerun of past shock.

Humans cannot commit such horrors without the ancient conditioning that helps convince people that war – especially if done in the name of God – is glorious.

Shortly before this book went to press, Steven Speilberg's film *Saving Private Ryan* opened in theaters. I saw it the first day it opened. I credit Speilberg for his courage to finally demonstrate in a film something close to what it was like for those soldiers who invaded Normandy in 1944.

Veterans of that war and especially the D-Day invasion praised Speilberg for being the first to portray what really happened that day. The first twenty-five minutes of the film is a graphic display of the horrors of war. A man has his arm blown off, and he retrieves it and carries it with him. A boy is screaming for his mother as his intestines lie strewed out over the beach. Many were shocked to see scenes of Americans shooting German soldiers who had their hands raised in surrender. This shocked people, but the veterans of the Normandy campaign know this happened.

In another very moving scene, men are struggling to save the life of one of their own. Tom Hanks as the captain has to make the tough decision whether to give morphine to a man who is in great pain. Everyone knows that he will die in minutes. The scene is pure minute-for-minute realism. No sanitized glory here.

Perhaps if some of this grit and realism had been in parts of the *Old Testament,* the taking of Canaan or the destruction of Jericho might not have been seen as glorious. I'm sure that the 180,000 men that Jehovah destroyed in another battle had mothers and fathers. I'm sure that those Egyptian soldiers who saw the Red Sea cascading back upon them experienced terror like they had never experienced in their lives.

But alas, they were on the wrong side.

As we proceed with this exploration of past shock, you will come to realize that no one was on the right side. Only an ancient conditioning that one was on the side of right could have kept such carnage continuing.

It is that ancient conditioning which keeps the carnage alive today. Most people know war is hell, but too many see it as a way to heaven. That lies deeply programmed within all of us.

The Modern Impact of Past Shock: Trust and Obey

In my youth, I found great joy in brainwashing myself with a favorite hymn called "Trust and Obey."

> Trust and obey
> For there's no other way
> To be happy in Jesus
> But to trust and obey.

If reincarnation is a reality, I am sure that some 4,000 years ago I might have found the same joy chanting "Fight and Obey." That was the consensus reality of the time. We dared not question.

We did not do this – nor do we continue to do so now – because we saw ourselves as a sin-bound, evil people. We did this then and continue to do this now because thousands of years ago we were intentionally conditioned to fight for an immoral group of beings that arrogantly called themselves gods.

In the beginning we didn't want to do this. We were naturally a peace-loving people. However, as we will eventually explore in this book, we are a genetically engineered species. We were bred first to toil and eventually to fight. If we resisted, the pretender gods got nasty.

The horror of this nastiness is buried deeply in our archetypal minds. This is the very foundation of past shock – something so horrible happened that we understandably want to block it out.

Psychologists go into great detail in psychological texts to explain how humans block out painful events from the past. The term for this is repression. A young girl who is repeatedly molested sexually by her father dissociates. That means that she – within her mind – creates another personality that simply observes herself being raped. This new personality becomes more dominant and eventually takes over because this appears to be the unharmed personality.

Sometimes a person being raped at a very young age will transfer the experience to something more bearable. Some will claim that they were abducted by aliens. They will claim that these aliens told them that they are special and have been chosen for a special mission. This way the abuse has a special meaning – something important, perhaps even holy.[2]

Julian Jaynes, author *of The Origin of Consciousness and the Breakdown of the Bicameral Mind,* claimed that this period thousands of years ago was a time of intense psychosis for the emerging human race. The entities that created this spiritual rape had no sense of honor, nor did they respect the sovereignty of the human race. Instead, they trained this emerging species to make war, to work hard for their masters, and eventually to worship them as God.

It was a horrible time. We are experiencing the severe fallout of those experiences today: past shock. Acts of individualistic belief were brutally punished. Daring to think that these "low life" beings were not God brought about the promise of everlasting damnation. Such thoughts also guaranteed misery for the rest of their earthly life – which often wasn't very long.

Future Shock and Past Shock

As mentioned previously, "future shock" is a term invented by author/researcher Alvin Toffler to describe people's inability to cope with changes that are moving too quickly into their experience. Presently, few people have a problem with understanding and accepting future shock. It is now part of the public lexicon and well-ingrained into American culture.

The only real relationship that future shock has to past shock is in the word "shock." In future shock, we have an anxiety about what is coming in our future. In past shock, we fail to reach our full potential as humans because of brutal shocks that we encountered in our past.

Past shock is not even close to being ingrained in the American paradigm. It probably won't for another ten to fifteen years. However, the fact that it is not a part of our collective paradigm does not mean it isn't impacting humanity. In fact, past shock is impacting humanity much more than future shock, and it has been doing so for at least 4,000 to 5,000

---

[2] This is not to suggest that everyone who thinks they've been abducted by aliens is a sexual abuse survivor. While many psychologists are comfortable with that theory, anyone exploring the alien abduction phenomenon (as I did in three separate articles for New Perspectives magazine) knows that this phenomenon just isn't that simple.

years. While some people have some understanding of future shock, only a slight minority of humanity has an understanding of past shock.

However, this millennial time promises to be an era when the realities of past shock will begin invading our comfortable reality. Then, the possibility and potential of the soul's true liberation will begin. In some very interesting ways it is beginning already. The popularity of all nine of Zecharia Sitchin's books[3] points to a significant shift in how we view our past.

Two of Sitchin's books – *The 12th Planet* and *Genesis Revisited* – are making the most impact. Both books expound the thesis that extraterrestrial visitors came to this planet 400,000 years ago from a large planet in our solar system. The planet Nibiru is in such extreme ellipsis that it comes into the solar system only once every 3,600 years. As Nibiru comes closer to the solar system, its inhabitants begin mining and colonizing the inhabitable planets. Evidently, Earth was their favorite planet. According to Sitchin, no human race as we know it now existed during the majority of those 400,000 years.

About 15,000 years ago, the gold that they were mining on Earth began to run out. The process of digging the gold became both laborious and dirty. The workers of Nibiru were on the brink of mutiny. The solution: create a worker race. According to Sitchin – and a host of other scientists who are starting to accept this theory – these extraterrestrial beings genetically spliced their own genes with the genes of Neanderthal Man, and created a worker race.

Past Shock will explore this aspect of the theory further in the book. Don't be concerned if this view deviates from the average human paradigm. It is much more frightening that an angry, jealous warrior God still remains within our collective paradigms.

A Past That Is Not Easily Embraced

I can understand that many readers reading this would put down the book and simply say, "This can't be." Yet the evidence of superior beings is woven into sacred, historical, and mythological texts. Most historians continue to hold onto the view that mythology was something made up by very creative minds. Yet, this consensus reality is increasingly failing to pass the reality litmus test. Claiming that the sacred texts are true and that mythological texts are fiction simply isn't logical: they are talking about the same events and the same beings.

---

[3] Zecharia Sitchin's books include *The 12th Planet, The Stairway to Heaven, Wars of Gods and Men, The Lost Realms, When Time Began, Genesis Revisited, Divine Encounters, The Cosmic Code*, and the synopsis of the first Sitchin Studies Day, *Of Heaven and Earth*.

The Sumerian god Enlil can't be fictional and the Hebrew god Jehovah be real when increasing evidence points to the fact that Enlil and Jehovah might be the same being. The flood created by Enlil and the flood created by Jehovah was the same flood. Scientific evidence now strongly asserts that a massive flood struck planet earth about 11,600 years ago. Yet this flood can't be the truth in the Bible and yet only a created fiction in the *Atra Hasis* and *The Epic of Gilgamesh*. With increasing evidence accumulating that Moses derived the early part of Genesis from the *Atra Hasis*, this separation becomes even more ludicrous.

If this working hypothesis of past shock is a reality, blocking out these memories does not serve us. If highly advanced beings did create us and then brutally exploited us, remaining in the dark about this doesn't help us. If we were so helpless in the presence of these awesome (and awful) beings, continuing to convince ourselves that this never happened will continue to keep us in the dark. All of this only helps us feel more comfortable as we stand in the path of increasing knowledge. Yet this false comfort will not set us free.

We collectively will continue to be crippled much in the same manner that people who block out past trauma are crippled. What we experienced at the hands of these beings was mental, emotional, and spiritual cruelty.

Science Provides Some Interesting Material

The *Old Testament* tells of Jehovah haranguing his people as they marched starving and terrified in their forty-year trek in the wilderness. The *Mahabharata* tells of Krishna goading a peace-loving Arjuna into fighting a bloody battle when he didn't have either the stomach or the motivation for it. Only Krisna's threat that his enemy would most likely use something with the power of a modern day atomic bomb caused Arjuna to give in and fight.

How interesting that traces of atomic radiation have been found on the site where this battle is alleged to have happened.

How interesting that traces of atomic radiation have been found at both the sites of Sodom and Gomorrah.

The ancient South American god Viracocha is alleged to have released a great explosion of fire in the sky to convince his constituents that he meant business. This caused terror in the people who observed, and they quickly behaved. How interesting that traces of atomic radiation have been found at this site in Peru.

Science becomes very interesting when it is set free from political agendas and limited paradigms.

The Bible Contains More Than Most Want to Accept

The first five books of the *Old Testament* tell of a covenant that promised starvation at such a level that eating one's sons and daughters would become necessary. Of course, all this could be avoided simply by obeying every one of Jehovah's commands. Failing to follow this "wonderful" covenant would result in sevenfold punishment. In that same portion of the *Old Testament* is the horrifying story of more than a thousand being killed by snakes tossed in by an angry Jehovah simply because of the Israelites' complaining that they were starving.

These are not the actions of a loving God. Instead, these are the actions of a "god" so brutal that if the same atrocities were inflicted on dogs in modern America, the perpetrator would have been reported to the ASPCA.

However, no Society for the Prevention of Cruelty to Humans existed on Earth thousands of years ago. These "wonderful gods" inflicted physical, emotional, and spiritual abuse with impunity. At that time we had no choice other than to endure and "go along to get along."

We were created as a worker race. We were created to be slaves. We were eventually conditioned to be "warriors for God." If we complained or rebelled, the punishment was severe and far in excess of the "crime."

This is what began as the foundation of past shock – being created as a worker race, being brutally and inhumanely exploited as workers, and then being brutally punished when we rebelled or dared to think for ourselves. These actions and the eventual rebellion to them laid the foundation for the creation of religion. If we tried to advance our knowledge beyond our "dumbed down" conditioning, we were harshly harangued and cruelly castigated.

Such was the case with Adam and Eve in the Garden of Eden. As will be covered in depth in Chapter Four, these two ancient humans did not fall, they did not create or indulge in original sin, and they are certainly not responsible for humanity's alleged "sinful condition."

Adam and Eve were courageous explorers who dared to leap to the next level of human growth. In Greek mythology the Titan Prometheus was seen as a benefactor to humanity. He and his brother Epimedius went up to Mount Olympus and stole fire from the Gods and gave it to humanity. This was an act of compassion. Yet Prometheus was brutally punished for this humane and compassionate act. Legend – or perhaps even history – tells that he was chained to a rock, and vultures tore out his liver every day. Because Prometheus was a Titan, he was able to heal his liver during the evening.

Could we still be so illogical in our thinking that we would think Jehovah and Adam and Eve were real people but that Prometheus and Epimedius were simply fictional mythological characters? Carl Gustav Jung claimed that humanity is still reeling from the Garden of Eden experience. The resulting archetype pervades both conscious and subconscious thought. Jung also suggests that the brutal punishment of Prometheus is a powerful archetype that lies deep within humanity's collective unconscious. These powerful archetypes from our collective unconscious (sometimes referred to as "racial memory") help us to believe that we were guilty because these "advanced beings" told us that is exactly how we should feel.

These pretenders – the pretender gods – were lying.

Moving from Past Shock to Future Potential

> One cannot escape from prison until he is
> willing to admit that he is indeed in prison.
>
> Georges Gurdjieff

Boldly exploring our ancient past is never easy. It is ugly, probably more ugly than we are capable of imagining. However, we will not move beyond our devastating conditioning until we accept that we were indeed conditioned. Most of the conditioning was lies:

> We are your God.
> You must worship us.
> If you work like a slave in this lifetime, you will get to rest for eternity.
> If you die fighting for us, you will go immediately to Paradise.
> You are creatures born in sin.
> We know what is best for you.
> Don't think for yourselves.
> You are most noble when you are working for us.
> To die gloriously is more important than living magnificently.
> You must continuously worship us.
> Avoiding this will endanger your mortal soul.
> I am the only true God. Don't even think about anything else.

The Pain of Waking up to Past Shock

Many will experience anguish as they begin to face the reality that the god or gods they have become comfortable with were not only *ungodly* but also were never God. Some will think that they are treading on the edge of blasphemy.

I certainly might have felt that if I had read this book twenty years ago. I would have been tempted to burn it and further fan the flames of my spiritual superiority complex. Some will feel that to read and consider the ideas presented in this book will be equivalent to deserting God. In reality, embracing the ideas in this book will help you to begin the process of embracing the true God.

Those who pretended to be God were responsible for the genetic engineering which moved ancient man (Neanderthals) to Cro-Magnon or modern man.[4] The important thing is that they did not create our souls! However, that did not stop these pretender gods from raping our souls.

Embracing this – or at least exploring its possibility – may be the most Godly thing you have done thus far in your life. Seeing Jehovah for what he really was might be frightening at first, but this clarity will eventually be liberating. Exploring the exploits of the Sumerian brothers Enki and Enlil may create some gasps of horror, but the knowledge of this horror will be the beginning of exploring and eventually eliminating past shock.

Accepting that the Greek gods like Zeus, Poseidon, and Dionysius might actually have been real beings who were a manipulative part of humanity's experience might be a giant step towards eliminating the impact of their brutal deeds. Whether you are a part of this experience or one who prays to be protected from the author's ideas, the discovery and eventual transformation of our past shock is beginning to gain momentum.

This will be an exciting time, but for many it will also be a terrifying time. (At the end of the book is an "Afterword" titled "Cracks in the Wall of Illusion." This will go into more detail about what is happening now to cause people to explore the possibility of past shock.)

The waking up to past shock will be more mentally unsettling than any potential mental unsettling described in Alvin Toffler's *Future Shock*.

What happened to us in the past is not pretty. Nor is it edifying. The concept of divine intervention will be seen in a totally different light. Killing people in the name of god will be seen for the cruel folly that it

---

[4] The term "modern man" will herein refer to mankind as we exist today, being the result of an incredible evolutionary leap engineered by an outside intelligence.

was. Looking forward to eternal rest will become less of a priority as present life becomes more meaningful and abundant.

I do not say this as some secular humanist hoping to destroy a person's religious faith. Instead, I say this as a person who has spent most of his life as an evangelical Christian. Moreover, I still see sanity in the ideas stated by Jesus Christ.

Where I will depart radically from the comfortable beliefs of Judaism, Islam, and Christianity is that I firmly believe that the increasing evidence from our past points to the reality that Jehovah was not God. Nor was he the father of Jesus Christ. The more deeply one probes into the evidence, the more some will come to the conclusion that Jesus Christ did not come to save us from sin, but instead he may have come to save us from Jehovah and the other pretender gods' conditioning.

For those of you who find these ideas offensive – perhaps even blasphemous – be aware that my intention is not to offend you or blaspheme against the true God. Sadly, that has already been done by Jehovah and the other pretender gods of ancient history.

Give Me That Old Time Brainwashing

Facing this potential reality will be difficult for many. Some will simply retreat more deeply into the depths of their ancient conditioning. Some will even reinforce this by brainwashing themselves in the same manner that the ancient humans were brainwashed thousands of years ago. However, facing this reality and exploring it further will aid individual humans and collective humanity on the path to spiritual liberation.

What – other than what we have discussed thus far – exactly was it that happened to collective humanity thousands of years ago? What was it that was so horrible that collective humanity finds blocking this reality easier than embracing it? What was so shocking that the human mind had to shield itself from it so that our everyday lives could avoid the stress of remembering?

The truth lies close by, so close that we have pushed what might liberate us into the realm of being a safety net that might eventually strangle us.

The Power of Myth and Ancient Writings

This truth which will eventually set us free lies in what is erroneously and safely called myth. Somehow calling our past history "myth" allows us to delude ourselves into thinking that what happened to us in the past was really something which was simply made up in people's heads.

How comforting.

How eventually destructive.

This liberating truth lies also within what we refer to as holy books. Within the *Old Testament*, The Hindu *Mahabharata*, The *Vedas*, The *Bhagavad Gita* (and many other holy books) lie clues to what really happened in our past.

Within the ancient classics like The *Iliad*, The *Odyssey*, The *Enuma Elish*, The *Epic of Gilgamesh*, The *Karsag Epics*, lie even more clues.

However, in the past we as a collective human species have been most reluctant to follow where these clues have been pointing. Instead, we have lulled ourselves into a collective aura of "myth is fiction." We have managed to convince ourselves that the writings of the ancient past are the creations of highly fertile minds fueled by wishful thinking rather than reality.

The Crumbling of the Pillars of Ignorance

Fortunately, and thanks to scholars who are beginning to embrace a more realistic paradigm, that reluctance is finally beginning to wane. With this waning, human beings singly and collectively have been looking at the clues and boldly inducing where the evidence is pointing. As mentioned before, some will approach this growing reality with great fear. Others find themselves like Darwin as he began making discoveries about the origin of the species. Darwin claimed, "With each new discovery I feel like I am committing murder."

So it is with me as the author. I grew up a comfortable and "certain" Christian. Now I face the horror of 5,000 –12,000 year old events and claim, "If these events are true, the foundations of our society will be rocked."

What is it that happened thousands of years ago that, when discovered, will rock the foundations of our society and cause the pillars of collective ignorance to collapse?

CHAPTER THREE

The Foundation of Past Shock

Close to 12,000 years ago a race of technically advanced beings were on this planet. According to researcher/author Zecharia Sitchin, these beings came here 400,000 years ago. The aforementioned mythology and holy books support this. More than 30,000 written documents from all over the world tell of a group of advanced beings who either came to Earth or were already living on Earth. Many of these documents – especially the Sumerian, Assyrian, and Babylonian writings – claim that these beings came to mine precious metals. (Whether they came from outside Earth, another dimension, or from another part of this planet is not really an important issue at this point in our exploration.)

As the precious metals became more depleted, the work became more demanding, and the miners became mutinous. The Sumerian holy book, the *Atra Hasis*, is amazingly clear in this area:

> Let us confront our chief officer
> That he may relieve our heavy work...
> Excessive toil has killed us,
> Our work is heavy, the distress much.
>
> Atra Hasis

In this amazingly complex ancient work, the *Atra Hasis* (along with other "mythological" works) relates accounts of long negotiations to prevent a bloody mutiny. Finally, the advanced beings decide on a solution to their problems:

> Let a Lulu [primitive worker] be created...
> While the Birth Goddess is present,
> Let her create a primitive worker.
> Let him bear the yoke...
> Let him carry the toil of the gods!
>
> Atra Hasis

Who was that primitive worker species? None other that what today is referred to as modern man. Where did these advanced beings get a

A stele apparently shows ancient deities tampering with the tree of life.

living species that would provide the basis for their "creation"? Being that these were not supernatural beings, they could not create something out of nothing. They needed to create their "worker being" from a species that was already roaming the earth.

In their search they had already determined that a species already on the planet was close enough to what they wanted. With some genetic engineering, they could create a hybrid species that they could condition and command as a work force. This species was already populating the planet in great numbers. We still refer to them as Neanderthals. After many false starts and corrections, what these advanced beings ended up creating is what history refers to as modern man.

What these advanced beings created was us. Yes, we are that species which was created to "do the toil of the gods."

We were created for one reason: to do slave labor.

However, as will be explored further on, the creation of religion would eventually become essential to keep humanity conditioned to be slaves.

As "far out" and paradigm-shattering as this theory appears to be, it does have one main area of scientific theory which will give it credibility. What has plagued scientists since the beginning of anthropology as a science is the "missing link" theory. According to this theory, another species should have logically been in between ancient and modern man. The quick leap from ancient to modern man is not biologically logical. The "missing link" – according the present scientific paradigm – would have to be a species that we have not found which would provide a logical transition from ancient man to modern man. However, if modern man (thousands of years ago) was a scientifically engineered species, then this not only explains the missing link, but it also explains why we have never found a missing link.

In the latter part of 1997, scientists after years of research have admitted that no genetic link exists between ancient man and modern man.

On the December 21, 1997, Art Bell Radio Show, scientific researcher Linda Moulton Howe claimed that scientists were facing the brutal reality that the human race may have emerged resulting from genetic engineering. The walls of the old paradigm are beginning to crumble.

The *Atra Hasis* claims that modern man was the result of a genetic splice between their genes and the genes of ancient man. The *Atra Hasis*, and other ancient writings, explain how the Anunnaki (as the gods were called in the Babylonian, Assyrian, and Sumerian epics) crossed its genes with the genes of an animal which most resembled them.

The Sumerian *Atra Hasis* and the Assyrian *Karsag Epics* along with the Sumerian *Enuma Elish* explain how the goddess Ninhursag allowed the eggs of an earthbound species to be placed in her womb. This happened after long periods of debate about whether the prime directive of not interfering with indigenous species should be violated. Only when the chief officers of the Anunnaki realized that they had a brewing mutiny on their hands did they agree to create this new worker species.

For millions of years Neanderthal man had no written language or a capacity for speech and language. Modern man had these skills almost immediately. According to the anthropology paradigm, this just isn't possible. However, if Neanderthal Man was indeed crossbred with an advanced humanoid species, this might explain why modern man became so skilled so quickly.

So, with all these wonderful gifts, why didn't things remain wonderful in paradise? Why wasn't our creation more of a joyful event instead of the hell on Earth that it quickly became?

Because modern man was a genetic cross between the old level of man and the gods, we turned out to be a very intelligent species – so intelligent that the Anunnaki's creations very likely threatened them. Because we were "born" a very intelligent species, we didn't take well to doing the menial work in the mines. We were much closer to being gods in those days than we are now. From the perspective of the gods, this "godliness" had to be drastically diluted. To insure that we would do their work with little or no resistance, we had to be dumbed down.

If only we had remained "good little workers" and stifled our god-like nature. Then, we could have avoided the wrath of the gods. However, we were precocious "children" who were both curious and rebellious, and these traits brought down the wrath of our creators. More like threatened parents than gods, they heaped large amounts of abuse upon us. In addition to abusive language and punishment, they eventually invented something that very effectively controlled us – religion.

As long as we believed our creators to be God, we could easily be manipulated. We could be led to believe that other more compassionate gods were actually evil. This might have been the case with Ba'al, the god whom Yahweh warned about worshipping. Ba'al evidently was the god of the peace-loving Canaanites, and the worship of Ba'al instead of

Jehovah apparently is one of the main reasons that Jehovah gave for the Israelites descending upon the Canaanites and committing the unjust carnage they inflicted upon the people of Canaan.

They had the wrong religion.

They didn't worship the spiritually correct god.

So wipe them out and take their land.

As the newly emerging humans justifiably began to question their gods, the creation of religious ritual was created. While many see the creation of the Sabbath as a holy day and a day of rest, others are beginning to get a different picture. Some historians are beginning to sense the creation of a rigidly enforced Sabbath might have been more of a brainwashing tactic.

Once a week the people would gather to praise a god whom many simply did not consider to be trustworthy. So many look upon Moses' angered smashing of the Ten Commandments as a justified act. How could his people build and worship a golden calf while he was up on the mountain talking to God Almighty? All the religious movies and sermons focus on Moses' despair.

However, focusing on something else might bring humanity closer to the truth.

What was going on in the people's minds that would cause them to depart from a God who was constantly in their presence. What did they know and what had they experienced that would create such despair that they would make an animal idol and worship that "graven image?" One needs to remember that the commandment to avoid making and worshipping graven images had not yet been presented to the Israelite people.

That commandment was lying in shambles, the result of a fit of temper by Moses. One wonders if Jehovah didn't insert this commandment after he saw what the Israelite people had done.

The rules of this newly created religion eventually became exceedingly oppressive. In a set of Jewish laws known as the *Mishna*, a pin that held clothing together could not exceed a certain weight. While the Israelites were in their long desert trek, Jehovah commanded a man to be stoned to death simply because he bent over to pick up a stick on the Sabbath. Amazingly, few people consider the act or the perpetrator of this act to be insane.

According to the prevailing mentality, this was an edict from God, and because it was an edict from God, it had to be followed. This resulted from the early stages of the creation of religion. Fear was the motivation, and obedience was the foundation. Disobey and you are sinning.

The concept of sin is one of the greatest victories of religion – present and past. Simply being born means you are already in deep trouble. Because of Adam and Eve, man is allegedly born in a state of sin. While many justifiably consider this idea to be patently absurd, this is the belief of the majority of people who are members of some of the major world religions.

This idea was a lie when it was presented to manipulate people in the name of God.

It is a lie today, and its manipulating impact can be devastating.

Yet it began with the early stages of creating a religion. Religion was created to "keep people in line." It may have begun with simple persuasion. However, as various humans saw through the sham created by the pretender gods, they understandably questioned and rebelled. With increasing human rebellion came the need of the pretender gods to manipulate and control in more effective ways.

Rituals were created to instill a brainwashing that discouraged open debate and spiritual exploration.

Rituals continue today. Some are inflicted upon the innocent at a very young age. This insures that belief systems rooted in "the truth" survive.

Religion today, as it did in history, often cannot allow exploration. Exploration would expose lies that are best hidden in the dark. Exploration would cause people to wonder why their parents continue to believe what they believe, and cause children to wonder why their parents didn't do some exploring on their own.

This is the tragedy of organized religion. While claiming to endorse free will, much of it all but discourages exploration. A tragic fallout from this conditioning is that it all but guarantees a person will be more centered in belief than experience. This is what the gods of ancient history realized. Experience was dangerous, exploration was dangerous, but religion insured that a certain belief system would be maintained.

We will explore further the impact of the created religions of ancient history. However, before exploring this further, we first need to understand what happened in this experiment which the gods were not counting on.

The Disastrous First Experiment

Like the disastrous "killer bee" experiment in South America more than thirty years ago, the genetic creation of humanity was not initially successful.

With the experiment that created the killer bee, the original intention was to cross the genes of a stronger bee with the genes of a bee that was more prone to work harder. Instead, what was created was a very rebellious bee with killer instincts and a strong tendency to migrate. What the pretender gods (the Anunnaki in Sumeria) wanted was a docile primitive worker who was smart enough to do menial work but not smart enough to know it that it was being exploited.

Like the killer bee, modern man turned out to be very bright, very innovative, and quite hostile to the idea of doing menial work. This initial group was bright – probably much brighter than we as humans are now. As a species we were so bright that we severely frightened our creators. They wanted us to do menial work in the mines, and we wanted to discover the secrets of the universe. We were like the precocious child who wanted to play with the chemistry set when Dad wanted us to mow the lawn. We wanted to be in the Chess Club when our parents wanted us to bring them glory by being a heavy hitter in Little League. The newly created humans were fascinated with the high technology of the all-powerful Anunnaki. However, the Anunnaki did not want us curious or smart. The wanted us to haul ore out of the mines without questioning their pretender god authority.

Yet, questioning their authority is exactly what the newly created humans did. The workers rebelled. While the new humans were impressed with the technology of their creators, they evidently were not impressed with their spiritual development. Evidently these precocious humans sensed that technologically evolved does not necessarily mean spiritual evolved. If humanity's creators had possessed more than a shred of spiritual development, they would have nurtured their newly created species from their inception.

However, their only intent was to exploit. They were more concerned with conditioning the new humans than helping them to advance as a species. Any feeling of warmth came from seeing these humans as pets rather than people. Getting arrogant or even indignant about this aspect really is not that productive. We treat our pets much in the same manner.

I gave my dog a bath whether or not she wanted it. I did not consult her as to why she ran under the bed every time I filled the washtub. Those who have their cats neutered really don't consider the feeling of the cat, despite the fact that being neutered can be a highly traumatic event.

Some people feel that swatting a dog for defecating on the rug is a justifiable act. Some go even further in their "motivation" of doggie ca ca placement by pushing the dog's nose into the offending effluvia. The trauma that this causes is not considered. The cleanliness of the new shag rug is the main issue. The self-esteem of the puppy is never considered. The issue is to get the dog housebroken.

Some might interpret this as a justification for what our creators did to us. This is not a justification. It merely points out that the people who have the power also have the "righteousness." Conditioning is accomplished by the strong, and the weak are the ones conditioned. Where humans differed is that they dared to resist. In contrast, the cat learns to live with being neutered and the dog eventually gets the idea through pain and inflicted guilt that defecating on the rug isn't a good idea.

We feel no shame when we take a horse that, in its early days would have preferred to run free in the wilderness, and domesticate it. People in other parts of the world feel no remorse when they make a water buffalo walk in a circle for twelve hours a day to keep water flowing into the fields. This is a mentality that we either inherited or had inflicted upon us. We like pets, and we don't like it when they express their free will in ways that makes life inconvenient for us.

Our creators must have felt the same way about us. We didn't like out pet status, *but they were the masters.* We wanted something better. Where we differ from other animals is that we were far more intelligent and were capable of sensing what was being done to us. We rebelled because it was in our nature to be free. Yet this was the last thing which our creators wanted for us.

Remember, we were created as a worker race.

Think of a group of workers at Taco Bell who were hired to make tacos and burritos as quickly as possible. However, these near minimum wage workers want to create a burrito that is nutritionally sound. Some of the workers even want to create tacos and burritos that will enhance the immune system. Others may want to create food that is more aesthetically prepared. One sweet young thing wants to create intellectually stimulating puzzles on the paper wrapper that surrounds the food. This drives the Taco Bell manager crazy. "Just make the goddam Taco!" he screams. "I didn't hire you to be creative." Thank God that we have so dumbed down our student population. Something like this occurring is highly unlikely.

However, during the early days of humanity, a time existed when we were not yet dumbed down. We rebelled against the idea of doing their dirty work. Eventually, these pretender gods upped the ante and wanted us to fight wars for them, and we rebelled against that. This is clearly recorded in the *Old Testament* and other ancient writings.

Was this compliance ensured by the time that the battle-obsessed Israelites descended upon the peace-loving Canaanites? This produced a carnage that resulted in a new land for these long-wandering Israelites. Perhaps it was sometime later when the war-obsessed Jehovah and the

42

Man was eventually taught to fight wars and slaughter the innocent.

decades-conditioned Joshua descended upon Jericho and slaughtered all of its people – warriors and innocent people alike. Anyone who reads these stories from the *Old Testament* and thinks that this represents something holy seriously needs to think for a moment and ask, "What's wrong with this picture?" But then one has to remember that Jehovah told Joshua to do this. Joshua can simply shrug his shoulders and say, "I was just following orders."

However, we have to be thankful for the good things. Both Jehovah and the Sumerian god Enlil didn't appear to be as obsessed with Earth women. That was more the pursuits of the Greek Gods. Dionysius couldn't leave Earth women alone, and he contributed to the misery of many human women who struck his fancy. Evidently, he created some joy too, but this is more likely from his accounting rather than the accounting of any women. But then Dionysius was mad (as in crazy). In one of the mind-raping rationalizations of past shock conditioning, we refer to the love-madness that Dionysius was having as "Divine Madness."

Well, thank God for that. Now we don't have to think of his acts as lechery – this was simply Divine Madness. Many a "dirty old man" would love that rationalization. Think how well that would play when a young eighth grade boy fresh off the start of puberty joyfully grabs the breasts of 15 of his female classmates before being restrained and sent packing. He puts his father at ease by claiming that "boys will be boys" and that he was possessed with Divine Madness. He explains that he should be praised for his spiritual advancement. He might even claim that he was a Tantra master in a previous life.

Maybe if Jehovah had had a little more passion for Earth women, he might have had less of an obsession for creating a plethora of holy wars. Of all of the hordes of material being written about history and mythology, no one has yet claimed that Dionysius and Jehovah were the same god.

This consistent theme of the gods fearing their own creations runs through all of the past writings from all parts of the world. We were smart.

Many of us might even have been smarter than our creators – and that must have severely frightened them. We started doing things that only increased their fears.

Another Version of the Tower of Babel

Zecharia Sitchin in *The 12th Planet* tells of a group of early humans in Babylon who were so intelligent that they built a rocket ship capable of escaping the Earth's orbit. (The *Atra Hasis* and other ancient epics state that these gods claimed to come from the stars.) The gods were terrified that their newly created species might get back to their (the gods') homeland and tell of this infraction of the prime directive. (The expression "prime directive" comes from the original 1960's *Star Treck*. The crew of the Enterprise were given strict orders not to interfere with the development of an emerging species.) Somehow this newly created human species sensed that the gods they were dealing with were the scum of their brood. They sensed that once they talked to the beings that these gods answered to, they might get better treatment.

Thus, the gods got together and worked out a plan to prevent this:

> Come, let us go down and con-
> found their language, that they
> might not understand one another's
> speech.

Genesis 11:7

Yes, according to Sitchin, the above is a much more accurate accounting of the Tower of Babel story than the tale of a group of "gone astray" humans who were simply trying to build a high tower in order to reach God. This is the commonly accepted Sunday school version. If God was already there in their presence, why did these humans feel a need to build a tower to get closer to God? This just doesn't compute.

Evidently, these early humans were not building a tower as much as they were building a launching pad. If this is true, then their getting free was something their creators simply couldn't allow. They came down upon these precocious beings brutally.

The horrors of past shock were increasing and intensifying.

Let's explore the *Old Testament* version in a little more depth. We are told in Genesis 11:1 that everyone spoke the same language. In verses 2-5, the early humans speak of building a city or a tower. The idea – according to the *Old Testament* – was that they would be able to ascend to the heavens. Then in verses 5 and 6, the Lord [the Elohim] came upon the scene and didn't like what he saw:

> And the Lord said, 'Behold the people are one, and they have all one language; and this they began to do; and now nothing will be restrained from them, which they have imagined to do.'
>
> Genesis 11:6

Here is another view:

> Look at this. Isn't it amazing what our human creations can do. Behold, they are independent and creative, and we glow with pride. Let's encourage them to develop their talents.

The first direct quote is of course from the book of "Genesis." The second quote represents what proud and emotionally secure creators would say about their new species. However, these words did not appear in "Genesis" – or the *Atra Hasis*. Our creators were emotionally depraved and spiritually bankrupt. They saw the rapidly increasing intelligence of their creations as a threat. Then, "the Lord" in all his "wisdom" and "compassion" creates such confusion that these humans can no longer communicate among themselves. This is recorded history's first intentional dumbing down.

How can anyone read this from the Bible and even dare to think that the true God could do such a heinous act? Is it Godly to wreak confusion and terror upon the human species? Is this what a loving God would do? Doesn't it say in First Corinthians 14:33 that "...God is not the author of confusion, but of peace...."?

Even by biblical and religious standards, this was a very cruel act. The true God – who is much more oriented toward creation than dogma and belief – would have applauded this act. However, the dreadfully insecure "creator gods" would of course have been threatened. This would have been the equivalent of the Taco Bell workers designing a more aesthetic looking Taco Bell building. As they are standing in awe of the blueprints of their new creation, the boss comes out and screams, "Get back inside and make burritos"!

It is not blasphemous to state that "the Lord" was uptight and overactive here. His human creations were of one mind and spirit. This should have been a cause for celebration. Instead, "the Lord" opted for kicking ass mightily and screamed "Get back into the mines and dig up some more ore." Years later "the Lord" would scream, "Get out on that battlefield and fight for me." Eventually, "the Lord would scream, "You better worship me as the true God, or I will really make it hot for you."

This being which the *Old Testament* refers to as "the Lord" was NOT God. This pernicious being was a pretender to the throne. He referred to himself as "the Lord" much in the same manner as a man or woman considers himself master of a dog. The "master" is stronger and more intellectually advanced. Therefore, the dog doesn't have much choice. It just hopes that it gets a master who is more nurturing than abusive.

One thing we can be sure of from both the *Old Testament* and the other holy books of the time. The newly created humans weren't being treated very well. Their working together as one was seen as a threat, and their punish-

Adam and Eve being expelled from the Garden of Eden.

ment was severe. If there is any truth to this unique interpretation of the Tower of Babel story, this is one of the most egregious infractions against any group of humans.

This, along with the Great Flood, must have been a great contributor to the collective human trauma that brought about humanity's past shock. However, before this building of the tower, another event happened which helped compound humanity's past shock and lay the foundation for the eventual creation of stultifying religious indoctrination.

Before the attempt to build the Tower of Babel, something even more brutal happened. This was something so severe that one might understand why the early humans might have been driven to [1] build a tower so high that they could reach into heaven or [2] build a rocket ship which would launch them free of what they saw as an oppressive planet. That previous event is what Swiss psychologist Carl Gustav Jung referred to as the most horrifying event in the racial memory of humanity – the experience of the "loss of paradise" from the Garden of Eden.

CHAPTER FOUR

Another View of the Garden of Eden Myth

What Really Happened in the Garden of Eden?

Freud, Jung, and other founding fathers of psychology claim that even if the events of the Garden of Eden myth didn't happen, its impact as myth is still a gaping wound in our collective consciousness. Author Richard Heinberg in *Memories, Dreams, and Recollections of Paradise* relates how human experience is shaped by our guilt for having been thrown out of the Garden of Eden. The accepted story is that God threw both of them out because they dared to eat of the Tree of Knowledge. This account goes on to state that this was the beginning of sin and where the fall of man began. Heinberg claims that this damaging guilt has been with us ever since.

According to many psychological interpreters of the human experience, the Garden of Eden experience has impacted humanity more than any experience in written history. In actuality, the consensus reality version of the story is one of the biggest lies ever inflicted upon humanity. Yet it lingers in many sincerely spiritual people's perception as truth.

Some go the circuitous route of claiming that the Garden of Eden story is a metaphor for some symbolic fall. This might make people feel better, but it does nothing but put a Band-Aid on a sore of bleeding guilt and provides a safe obfuscation for one of the most powerful moments of past shock.

The problem with the prevailing consensus reality about the events of the Garden of Eden is that it is wrong and highly manipulative. Its source of knowledge is tainted by the erroneous belief that the being or beings who threw Adam and Eve out of the Garden of Eden were God. The true God would never insist that one of his creations limit his or her knowledge. The true God is a God of unlimited potential and unbounded creativity. God would never have been so petty as to insist that one approach the increase of knowledge as something forbidden or sinful.

The true God might have even suggested eating of the Tree of Knowledge – albeit with some cautious suggestions. However, this true God would never have lied to His people about death being the result of the act of eating from the tree. As we shall soon see, the serpent was the one who told the truth, and "God" was the one who lied when he claimed that "...you shall surely die if you eat of the tree." As far as inflicting pain or punishment, the true God would find this both useless and counterproductive. However, what humanity had to contend with in ancient history was a group of pretender gods – gods who claimed they were gods only because they were technologically superior and this gave credence to their claim.

We bought it.

Tragically, most of us are still buying it.

However, being technologically advanced has never meant being spiritually advanced.

What the events of the Garden of Eden were, in reality, was the beginning of a spiritual rape from which we are still suffering (or at least blocking out). We still continue to see as divine those who spiritually raped us. We rationalize that "God in His wisdom" did what was best for humanity.

Not true! The pretender gods, in an egregious lack of wisdom, brutally abused our fragile and growing spiritual psyches by dumping a devastating load of excessive and unjust guilt upon us. Most of us continue to experience that guilt today – even those who do not believe the Garden of Eden story. Some within the more conservative structures of organized religions actually salivate for the opportunity to wax lyrical about what sinful creatures they are. The pretender gods did their job well. They did not respond in a spirit of love, but instead reacted in a manner that was exploitative and guilt inducing.

The Garden of Eden event was one of the strongest moments of past shock. Most likely, this event did actually happen. This is not some metaphor of myth thought up by overactive ancient minds. Denying this by pushing it into the safety of metaphor may be safe, but it is not productive. Spiritual growth does not come from intellectually trivializing events simply because they cannot be grasped or understood.

This event made the pretender gods realize that they were going to have to find more "sophisticated" ways of manipulating us. This would eventually lead to the creation of religion and the spiritual holocaust perpetuated by Jehovah and the Elohim (the plural name for God used in early portions of the Bible).

(At this point a clarification is essential. Some biblical scholars claim that it was the Elohim who brought about the tragedy of the Garden of Eden. This would refer to a group of gods rather than just one God. Others claim that Jehovah, because he is allegedly eternal was the singular God who was in the Garden of Eden. For the rest of this chapter I will refer to Jehovah as the one who banished Adam and Eve from the Garden of Eden. I am aware that some Bible scholars will have problems with this.)

The conditioning of ancient humans to believe that Adam and Eve are responsible for our allegedly sinful nature is one of the biggest "con jobs" ever foisted on the human race. Just because this idea was conditioned over and over in our psyches does not make it true.

Adam and Eve – Sinners or Heroes?

Adam and Eve were pioneers in the emerging human experience. They were both courageous and compassionate. Like Prometheus, the Titan who brought fire to humanity, they paid dearly for their courage. What "the Lord" did to them was neither just nor appropriate. It was spiritual rape.

While it is both safe and often politically correct to relegate the Garden of Eden story into the realm of myth, such action continues the enslavement and conditioning of past shock. It does nothing to help humanity break free of it. Something did happen in the Garden of Eden – something very horrible. One of the gods – a pernicious pretender to divinity who called himself Yahweh (Jehovah) – got totally caught up in his perverse paternalism and decided that Adam and Eve would be better off as cosmic pets. They would be totally dependent on their masters with no free will. Their needs would be provided for as long as they remained at the "domesticated" level.

Into the picture came a creature that figured Adam and Eve were getting a bad deal. This creature believed that Adam and Eve were intelligent c reatures who were being told to keep their lights hidden under a bushel. Throughout history this creature has been greatly maligned. Some even claim that it was Lucifer, but not even the *Old Testament* calls this creature by that name. In the Bible this creature was simply referred to as the Serpent. In the majority of mythology and holy writings the Serpent was

In China, serpents and dragons were seen as beneficial creatures.

known as the purveyor of wisdom. The Chinese saw both serpents and dragons as godlike, beneficial creatures that advanced humanity.

However, the serpent gets very bad press from the Judeo-Christian segment of humanity. The majority of people in the Judeo-Christian community continue to see the serpent as evil, perhaps even the devil. About the only thing that mythological writings and holy books like the *Old Testament* do agree upon is that the serpent was very beautiful – and very wise.

Considering this fact, it is amazing how much of the original story is left in the *Old Testament*.

The King James Version of the *Old Testament* has "Eve deceived" and "The Fall of Man" as headings to Chapter 3 of Genesis. As a young boy and a maturing adult, I was programmed by these overt editorializations. How nice it would have been if the headings had been a little closer to the truth:

"Eve Inspired"
"The Liberation of Humanity"

However, the people who wrote the *Old Testament* – and too many of those who followed as translators – were more conditioned as to what to write rather than being divinely inspired. The headings in the King James version of the *Old Testament* point out how this conditioning was still running strong in 17th century England. While still running strong today in collective humanity, that conditioning is finally beginning to unravel.

A Fresh Look at an Old Story

Let's look more closely at the Garden of Eden Story:

And the Lord God planted a garden eastward in Eden; and there he put the man he had formed.
And out of the ground made the Lord God to grow every tree which is pleasant to the sight and good for food; the tree of life also in the midst of the garden and the tree of knowledge of good and evil.

Genesis 2: 8-9

Thus we have established the source of the problem: the Tree of Knowledge. What does the Lord God do? He puts it right in the middle of the garden. If you have a hungry dog and you have a $75.00 birthday cake fresh from the bakery for you mother's birthday party, would you put the cake in the middle of the floor? We have a crisis of wisdom here.

But hang on: the story gets "better":

> And the Lord God commanded the man say-
> ing, "Of every tree of the garden thou
> mayest freely eat.
>
> But of the tree of knowledge of good and
> evil thou shalt not eat of it, for in the day
> thou eatest thereof thou shalt surely die."
>
> Genesis 2: 16-17

Now imagine that I have this dog called Sappho, and I spread a whole bunch of dog food around. I say, "Now, Sappho, you can have all you want of the Grow Pup. You have lots of Milk Bones here. But you see that birthday cake in the middle of the floor? You touch that, and it's your ass." Is there any dog owner on planet earth who would do anything so stupid? I can hear it now: "I have a good doggie who does exactly what I say. There's no way that my sweet little hound is going to eat the birthday cake."

The Lord God of the *Old Testament* – according to the accepted paradigm – was omniscient, omnipotent, and omnipresent. In other words, He was allegedly a highly advanced being. Why is a highly advanced being putting a forbidden fruit right in the middle of the garden? If this Lord God was indeed omniscient, he knew in advance that Adam and Eve were going to eat from the forbidden tree.

Some of the Protestant sects would claim that this was predestined, which would make this "Lord God" even more cruel. If this "Lord God" knew this in advance, why didn't he take the tree and put it in another garden? After all, he was allegedly God and had just finished creating the Earth. This couldn't have been that much of a task.

After setting up (in more ways than one) Adam in the Garden of Eden, the "Lord God" decides that living alone isn't a good idea for Adam. He creates Eve – the first woman. The point is made that Adam and Eve were naked and they were NOT ashamed.

All of a sudden another creature enters the scene: the Serpent. We have no preparation for this. Since the "Lord God" created everything, the serpent must be one of his creations. But he was a unique creation:

> Now the serpent was more subtle than any
> beast which the Lord God had made. And
> he said unto the woman, "Yea, hath god said
> 'Ye shall not eat of every tree of the gar-
> den.?'

52

And the woman said unto the serpent, 'We may eat of the fruit of the trees of the garden.

But the fruit of the tree which is in the midst of the garden,' God hath said, 'Ye shall not eat of it, neither shall you touch it, lest ye die.' "

And the serpent said unto the woman, "Ye shall not surely die.

For God doth know that in the day ye eat thereof, then your eyes shall be opened, and ye shall be as gods, knowing good and evil."

Genesis 3: 1-4

As mentioned before, Jesus emphatically stated "Do you not know that you are gods"? Does this mean that Jesus is more like the Serpent than Jehovah? If as most commonly accepted wisdom states, that Jesus was the son of Jehovah, maybe he was adopted. How come this little "Ye are Gods" morsel from the *New Testament* rarely shows up in a church sermon? How come Jehovah is saying one thing and Jesus is saying something that directly contradicts it?

Adam and Eve being tempted by the serpent to partake of The Tree of Knowledge.

Do we have a father and son conflict here?

Another very important fact needs to be established. When the "Lord God" claimed that Adam and Eve would die if they ate of the fruit from the forbidden tree, the "Lord God" was lying. Both ate of the fruit, and they did not die. Thus, the serpent was telling the truth. How does this reality concur with the consensus reality that claims that the "Lord God" was good and the serpent was evil?

Is it possible that the serpent was a force of liberation trying to help liberate Adam and Eve from a highly oppressive "Lord God"?

Consider this. Jehovah tells Adam and Eve that they can have everything they want as long as they don't eat any fruit from the Tree of Knowledge. This is the equivalent of being told that you can have everything you want as long as you don't expect more than minimum wage and don't complain about the working conditions. Isn't it counterproductive to human growth to forbid something that will advance human growth?

The serpent tells them that if they eat of the fruit of the Tree of Knowledge, their knowledge and perception will increase significantly. At this point, the serpent is like Prometheus who is about to steal fire from the gods. As mentioned before, the serpent is telling the truth. Its aim is not to destroy Adam and Eve as much as to liberate them.

What happened to Adam and Eve would appear to be good, if it didn't have the "evil" spin perpetuated by the *Old Testament*:

> And when the woman saw that the tree was good for food and that it was pleasant to the eyes, and a tree desired to make one wise, she took of the fruit thereof and did eat and gave also unto her husband with her; and he did eat.
>
> And the eyes of them were both opened, and they knew that they were naked; and they sewed fig leaves together and made themselves aprons.
>
> And they heard the voice of the Lord God walking in the cool of the day. And Adam and his wife hid themselves from the presence of the Lord God amongst the trees of the garden.
>
> And the Lord God called unto Adam and said unto him, "Where art thou?"
>
> Genesis 3: 6-9

What? Wait a minute! Something's wrong with this picture! Why is this alleged omniscient, omnipresent "Lord God" asking Adam where he is hiding? If he is everywhere (omnipresent), he is already where Adam is hiding. If he is all knowing (omniscient), he should immediately know where Adam is hiding. Could it be possible that this "Lord God" was not actually God?

Also, if Adam and Eve are experiencing a greater clarity, what's the problem. Okay, Adam is all of a sudden embarrassed about his penis and Eve feels she needs to cover her breasts and other genitalia. Most advancement in knowledge has some negative side effects. The bottom line is that despite feeling some shame about their nakedness, both felt that they had experienced something wonderful. Adam did run and hide, but that was most likely from his remembering that the "Lord God" made it very plain that eating of the Tree of Knowledge was a no-no.

Ethnobiologist/author Terence McKenna has a very unique and controversial theory about this experience in the Garden of Eden. McKenna believes that humanity was advancing at a sane rate, thanks mainly to the discovery and ingestion of psychedelic compounds like psilocybin mushrooms. Then "God" came along and stopped it because "He" felt that humanity was advancing too quickly. Adam and Eve had taken some substance that significantly increased the clarity of their knowledge and perception. "God" basically said, "That's as far as you go, and I'm going to get mean because you dared to go this far." McKenna refers to the Garden of Eden experience as "God's big drug bust."

Admittedly, Terence McKenna is a very controversial writer and lecturer. Some students of mine have written papers (based on a magazine article of mine) about Terence McKenna. Some genuinely believe that he is the anti-Christ. Not only is this a ridiculous – and highly conditioned – reaction to McKenna's ideas, but it also begs the question of exploring his ideas. As controversial as they are, McKenna's ideas may be closer to the truth than those stated in the biblical account. Our programmed conventional wisdom from the past may not hold up under scrutiny.

The only way the "Lord God" could have been threatened by Adam and Eve's increased clarity was if this increased clarity would have made it more difficult to treat humanity as cosmic beasts of burden. Because at least the first six chapters and other material from Genesis were taken from the *Atra Hasis* and other Sumerian sacred books, one might understand this theory more clearly.

The *Atra Hasis* states very clearly that the human race was created as a worker slave race. It also points out with great clarity that this newly created race was very intelligent and quite rebellious. Wanting to explore ways to greater clarity and knowledge was most likely in-bred into us. (This certainly was not the case with Neanderthal Man.) In one of history's cruelest ironies, the newly created humans might have been brutally punished because they dared to be like the beings that created them.

Yet, humanity's creators did not appreciate this curious striving. These pretender gods wanted to squelch this curiosity and return humans to the state of semi-intelligent beasts of burden. This is pointed out in greater detail with the Mayan *Popul Vuh* in the next chapter. These pretender gods stopped at nothing to bring us back to a more manageable status. This included brutal punishment and the eventual creation of religion.

What followed in the Garden of Eden story contributed greatly to our past shock:

> And the Lord God said unto the serpent,
> "Because thou hast done this, thou art cursed
> above all cattle and above every beast in
> the field; upon thy belly shalt thee go, and
> dust shall thou eat in the days of your life.
>
> And I will put enmity between thee and the
> woman, and between thy seed and her seed;
> it shall bruise thy head and thou shalt bruise
> his heel."
>
> Genesis 3: 14-15

Despite the fact that the "Lord God" had recently created Eve, he evidently forgot her name and kept referring to her as "the woman." What Adam and Eve did not forget was the brutal trashing of the Serpent. Other holy books describe an even more horrific fate for the serpent. Books like the Jewish *Pseudepigrapha* and *The Secret Book of John the Gnostic* tell of the Serpent's brutally having each of its limbs hacked off.

Such a loving act for this "Lord God."

It gets worse:

> Unto the woman he said, "I will greatly mul-
> tiply thy sorrow and thy conception. In sor-
> row thou shalt bring forth children.
>
> Genesis 3: 16

Now there's a real divine manifestation of a loving and merciful "Lord God." In essence, this egregious pretender god was saying that not only was he going to "kick ass" mightily, but that he was going to do it in such a way that every time that a woman had a child, she would experience this same pain.

How wonderful.

This is not a godly manifestation or a decree uttered by God. It was instead the fruition of a very sick mind that played at being God and, quite frankly, did a very poor job of it.

This sick pretender god wasn't finished:

> And unto Adam he said, "Because thou hast
> harkened unto the voice of thy wife and hast
> eaten of the tree, of which I commanded thee

> that thou should not eat of it; cursed is the
> ground for thy sake; in sorrow shall you eat
> of it all the days of thy life.
>
> Thorns and thistles shall it bring forth to
> thee, and thou shalt eat of the herb of the
> field.
>
> In the sweat of thy face shalt thou eat bread,
> till thou return to the ground; for out of it
> wast thou taken: for dust thou art, and unto
> dust shalt thou return.
>
> Genesis 3: 17-19

This "Lord God" was obviously very angry. More accurately, he was out of control, much in the manner that someone flagrantly beats a dog into painful submission because the dog dared to chew on its master's favorite pair of slippers. The dog may have been wrong for chewing up the slippers, but beating it mercilessly because of "justified" anger is a severe overreaction. Now imagine that this hostile master kicks the dog out of the house and posts two Cherubim with flaming swords [Genesis 3: 24] outside the doggie door to insure that this "sin-bound" dog never gets back in.

Wouldn't that also be just a little bit excessive? Couldn't a case be made for overreaction? What exactly was it that caused the "Lord God" to go in such a fitful rage?

> And the Lord God said, "Behold, the man
> has become one of us, to know good and
> evil, and now lest he put forth his hand and
> take also of the tree of life and eat and live
> for ever."
>
> Genesis 3:22

Okay, now a little bit of "understanding" enters the picture. This cosmic beast of burden has gone too far. Thanks to ingestion of the fruits of the Tree of Knowledge, the cosmic beast of burden – this slave created for menial work – now dares to think that it's something more than a slave.

This new creation dares to think that it might be equal to the pretender gods.

Bad Doggie!!!

The pretender gods couldn't have that. They would have to thump this collective human race, and thump it hard.

Continuing the dog analogy, it isn't very hard to make a dog feel guilty (unless you own a poodle). All any human has to do is inflict enough well timed verbal or physical pain on the dog, and the dog will quickly think that something is wrong with it. What the dog wants is for the pain to stop. Therefore, it can be conditioned with pain. Also, a dog can be made to feel guilty about doing things which displease its master: crapping on the rug, chewing up the bed spread, barking at three in the morning. Like dogs, humans not only do guilt very well; they might do it better than any other animal species.

The Garden of Eden was the beginning of intense guilt for the emerging human race. And this excruciating guilt is a solid foundation for past shock. Thousands of years later we still have it. The pretender gods who inflicted us with this guilt were not anything close to being the true God. The true God would never use guilt to motivate its creations. Moreover, a part of us exists which is free of guilt. This part needs to be nurtured.

However, the pretender gods were frightened. They had to go back to the drawing boards and refine the emerging humans. Once refined, these pretender gods would need to create a kind of control mechanism that would condition humans to revere and obey the pretender gods.

What they did was very effective – and very cruel.

CHAPTER FIVE

Back to the Drawing Boards
The Spiritual Rape Intensifies

Before moving to the next level of this exploration, a few ideas by two other highly respected authors are appropriate. While admitting that the expulsion from paradise was traumatic, authors Ken Wilber and Rollo May argue that the Garden of Eden experience was the beginning of humanity's liberation. The title of Ken Wilber's excellent book *Up From Eden* points out his thinking. What happened in the Garden of Eden was not a fall, but instead a step upward? Rollo May in *The Courage to Create* uses the expression "Adam and Eve fell upward." What Adam and Eve saw as a fall – because of the dreadful manner in which they were punished – was instead a giant step forward for humanity. We went from being docile pets and began the march toward becoming creative human beings.

Ideas like Wilber's and May's are no longer considered that revolutionary. Thinking that Adam and Eve "fell" is an idea whose time is starting to fade. Blaming Adam and Eve for the "sinful nature of man" is still lodged in the thoughts of a majority of religious people. However, that wall of thought is also beginning to crumble. Even among fundamentalist groups of the three major religions, some are beginning to ask some probing questions:

> 1) If God is all knowing and knew that Adam and Eve were going to pollute the human race, why didn't he stop it?
> 2) If Jehovah was indeed God, why did He lie to Adam and Eve about the fruit of the Tree of Knowledge creating death?

In weighing the intentions of the serpent and Jehovah, which one most wanted the spiritual liberation of humanity?

We are only a few years away from increasing numbers of spiritual seekers exploring the idea that Adam and Eve might have been set up.

Jehovah was not a mentally healthy being. He loved war, he was exceedingly jealous, he was excessively territorial, and he often extracted punishment far in excess of the crime. A thorough reading of the *Old Testament* does not portray Jehovah as a divine being as much as it portrays a being harboring borderline psychotic behavior.

The expulsion from the Garden of Eden is most likely the prime moment of humanity. To please this highly unstable Jehovah, Israelites had to (1) fight wars they often didn't want to fight, (2) march around in the desert for forty years while the planet was going through some terrifying earth changes, and (3) encounter the punitive wrath of Jehovah for ridiculously small offenses.

The majority of the most emotionally unstable dog owners would not treat their dogs with the cruelty that Jehovah treated the Israelites. Like a collective battered child, the Israelites were mentally, physically, and unjustly savaged by a jealous, ultra-territorial punk who ranted and raved and slaughtered at will. Thank God that Jehovah didn't like women, or he probably would have raped the more nubile of the Israelite women.

Fallout from the Pretender Gods Punishing Their Own Gods

However, *Old Testament* apocryphal books tell of Jehovah coming down very hard on those "sons of God" who dared to comingle connubially with the "daughters of men." *The Book of Enoch* relates horrifying "tours" which the pretender gods gave to Enoch showing the severe punishment given to members of their own tribe who broke their established laws. Often Enoch saw areas of flames and oppressive gasses that were inflicted upon those "sons of God" who dared have sexual relations with the daughters of the newly created humans.

Here is a new view of these circumstances. If some ancient sexual harassment occurred on the part of the pretender gods, it was not just the pretender gods who were punished:

> And to Gabriel, the Lord said: "You must take action against the bastard children who have become reprobates – the children of fornication. Destroy all children of the Watchers [the Anunnaki]; set them against one another so that they will kill each other in battle; for they shall not have long life. And no pleading which fathers shall make shall be listened to....
>
> And when their sons have killed each other and they have witnessed the destruction of their loved ones, imprison them for seventy

> periods in the valleys of the Lowlands until
> their day of trial. Then they shall be led off
> to the ravine of fire where they will be im-
> prisoned for life."
>
> *The Book of Enoch* 10: 1-12

While some might sense that "the Lord" is trying to keep the pretender gods away from the "inferior" Earth women, the cure is both devastating and unjust. Wars will be created so that these "bastards" will kill
each other. These "bastards" did not ask to be born. Their only sin was
that they were the spawn of a connubial binding between a horny pretender god and a human woman. Yet, the horror of slaughter and the pro-
jected guilt of being "less than perfect" must have burned itself into the
awareness of the newly created humans. According to psychologists like
Carl Gustav Jung and historical writers like Julian Jaynes, this archetypal
memory lies deep within us and still impacts humanity today.

Our views of hell as a place of flames and smoke may come from this
archetype.

Our views of hell may be more grounded in past conditioning than
any present reality.

The use of hell as a threat and motivating force by many major religious sects points out that using this fallout from the past may very effective – even if it isn't very honorable.

According to *The Book of Enoch*, the flood was created to rid the
earth of this bastard spawn.

The Origins of Hell

However, Enoch was fortunate. He was one of the rare newly created
humans who was revered and trusted by the pretender gods. Blessed with
the skill of dramatic and effective writing, Enoch was taken to from the
high courts of the Anunnaki to the pits of the punished. Even writer/re-
searcher Christian O'Brien believes that even this contributed to
humanity's conditioning. He supports the idea that the accounts of the
flaming and noxiously gaseous areas of punishment were so vivid that
they most likely have contributed to our fearfully twisted version of hell:

> And from there I went to a place that was
> even more horrible, and I saw another fear-
> ful thing a great fire which burned and
> blazed in a place that was cleft down to the
> bottom of the ravine, full of great, falling
> columns of fire. I could neither see its size
> or its extent; nor could I even guess at them.

> I said, "How fearful is this place, and how
> terrible to look at."
>
> *The Book of Enoch* 20: 7-9

Enoch was looking at a guided tour of the place the "angels" were sent. Those who dared to mate with human women were sent to a horrible place for punishment. Enoch's guide claimed that these "angels" would be imprisoned in this hell for life. Since these angels allegedly lived for periods of 10,000 to 100,000 years, this was a most harsh punishment and may have contributed to humanity's concept of eternal damnation.

Yet, even when Enoch was with "the good guys," he was still terrified:

> And I entered that house, and it was as hot
> as fire and as cold as ice, and it was devoid
> of comfort, and I began to panic again, and
> to tremble.
>
> *The Book of Enoch* 16: 13-14

This last description is of a "very high up" member of the Anunnaki who actually appreciated Enoch for his ability to write and communicate with people of his own race. Reading his descriptions not only points this out but also makes the reader aware of his terror about what he was observing. If he was making this up, where was he getting his "inspiration"?

If Enoch's skills were appreciated, this was one of the rare exceptions in the gods' relationship with their created humans. All of the "mythological" accounts suggest that the first humans were very intelligent and very creative. And this did not please the pretender gods. The pretender gods did not want creative human beings. Nor did they want spiritually advanced humans.

They wanted a "worker slave" which would do what it was told... without question. These pretender gods wanted a creature that could be conditioned to work hard and efficiently without complaining. Unfortunately for the pretender gods that is not what the first brood of humans turned out to be.

The Gods Become Tired of Their Own Creations

One theme stands out in the thousands of mythological and holy writings: our creators didn't like us as they originally created us. We were too smart. From their perspective we were also too arrogant. We initially refused to become domesticated. We complained incessantly. The *Atra Hasis* tells of one of the gods who has had enough:

The god Enlil said to the other gods:

> "Oppressive have become the pronounce-
> ments of Mankind. Their conjugations de-
> prive me of sleep."
>
> *Atra Hasis*

Being old enough to have suffered through three years of Latin studies in high school, I found a perverse humor in the term "conjugation."
However, Enlil (who some scholars have claimed was Jehovah) sees no
humor in the wailing pronouncements of his newly created worker race.
Something must be done. A new and more refined creation is needed: a
dumbed down worker human. Our creators had already created spiritual
rape by advancing us too quickly; now they were going to "de-advance"
us.

This also added to the foundation of our past shock. As a species, we
did not have the advantage of advancing at a normal rate. As an ancient
version of man, we were abruptly jump-started into modern man. One
only need think about the passages of life in humans. Adolescence and
mid-life crisis can be turbulent enough in the normal flow of the human
seasons. However, to be rapidly advanced and then dumbed back down?
This amounts to spiritual, emotional, and physical rape. We were "jerked
around" at someone else's pleasure much in the same manner that we
treat animals that we are going to use or eat.

We were not consulted.

We were simply used.

Some Devastating Conditioning about Sex

The impact of all of this has created a highly unstable species that
desperately wants to do well but carries around conditioning that says
fighting in holy wars will lead to paradise and the sex drive is evil. This
sex drive was in itself brutal. Jehovah claimed that this sex drive, as powerful as it was, was to be used only for creating life.

More truthfully in the context of these times, this meant using sex
mainly to generate more slaves. Jehovah's desire was that someone would
only be able to have sex if it was used in the production of more and more
worker slaves. If your pleasure did not have as its goal the creation of
more humans, it was then considered a sin.

What is tragic is that this totally unworkable idea is still the foundation for sexual mores in much of the world. No matter how powerful the
sex drive (usually beginning at ages 10-13), it still must be contained
until one marries and is producing new bodies for the mining machine.

No wonder sexual confusion is the order of the day.

The onslaught of AIDS and other sexually transmitted diseases has only added to the confusion and intensified the anguish of the human experience.

Brutally effective conditioning from the past helped us to believe that this powerful sex drive must be contained within strictly moral and often stultifying codes. This was most likely done to keep our very bored human species from breeding too quickly. What is most amazing is that few question the sanity of a "deity" who creates a very powerful sex drive and then makes rules about how it must be ridiculously sublimated.

Having a fully blown sex drive and not being able to express oneself sexually until one is married ten years later can be exceedingly frustrating. Add to this the overt stimulation of sex on television and in feature films, and the temptation is exacerbated. Doing time on planet Earth can be maddening.

Deeper within this awful conditioning is the promise of Paradise – if only one will sacrifice one's needs and desires in this life. The awesome effects of this show up strongly in the workplace where workers show a perverse loyalty to employers who haven't a shred of loyalty to those who work for them.

Dumbing Down Humanity

The gods were mentally imbalanced Rodney Dangerfield types who felt they just didn't get enough respect. Jehovah, Enlil, Zeus, Wotan – not only did they want workers who didn't complain, they also wanted their newly created humans to venerate and revere them. While this is also a dominant theme in ancient writings, the one sacred book that best describes this is the Mayan sacred book The *Popul Vuh*. This holy book not only tells how the gods created humans as a work force, but also points out how these gods had to keep recreating humanity:

> We have already tried with our first cre-
> ations, our first creations, our first creatures,
> but not make them praise and venerate us.
> So let us try to make obedient, respectful
> beings who will nourish and respect us.
>
> *Popul Vuh*

Thus, halfway around the world in Central America another group of gods was severely distressed with what they had created. Writing this off as "merely mythology" may create a "safe" certainty. However, it also keeps humans in a state of denial about what really happened to them in their ancient past. If this is indeed a reality, keeping these events buried in ignorance is eventually going to create even more suffering. Modern psychology reveals that keeping trauma repressed creates a lack of mental health and the building of unbearable tension.

A person who has been through trauma – and is now coming to realize it – needs the gentle and effective guidance of a therapist to bring the trauma to the light. That is eventually what collective humanity is going to have to do in facing its own past shock.

Could it be that we actually turned out to be more intelligent than our creators? Is it possible that we were abused because we refused to act like domesticated beasts of burden – that we only acted... well, human?

According to the *Popul Vuh*, the dumbing down worked (in this case after five previous ineffective experiments). What exactly was it that they were trying to dumb down? What exactly was the result of these ongoing experiments?

> ...they saw and they instantly could see far,
> they succeeded in seeing, they succeeded
> in knowing where all is in the world. When
> they looked, they saw instantly all around
> them, and they contemplated in turn the arch
> of the heaven and the round face of the earth.
>
> *Popul Vuh*

Was it for this that we needed to be dumbed down? Could this have been what frightened our creators and led them to perform a devastating act? We were genetically engineered and conditioned from birth to be creatures which would venerate and worship those who created (and spiritually raped) us. The *Popul Vuh* states how the gods were finally "victorious" in getting us to be obedient workers who worshipped our genetic creators.

Other than having the divine seed that all humans have, there was little which was godly or divine about these creators. They were liars who were bored, and they used us as play-fodder. They demanded worship because their souls were spiritually undeveloped. Being worshipped pleased them much more than pursuing spiritual growth.

They made us fight their wars because they lacked the resolve and courage to fight them on their own They apparently lacked even the wisdom to prevent wars from breaking out among themselves. They made us build large edifices to praise them when they weren't even close to being worthy of praise.

We believed all of this because we had been so dumbed down that we no longer had the capacity to question those who committed this spiritual rape. We worshipped them because they treated us quite brutally if we didn't. We fought their wars because we knew that we would be slaughtered if we refused. We praised them because that was what kept them calm. They got quite nasty if they didn't get what they wanted.

Conditioning Humans to Condition Themselves

With every veneration and praise, we etched into our cellular conditioning that these pretenders were God. We must have known that this was a sham because – despite all the conditioning and dumbing down – we often resisted valiantly. Jehovah kept the Israelites in the wilderness for forty years so that he could condition a generation of killer warriors.

At the end of this forty-year period, they had no complaining Moses and no questioning Aaron. Now they had Joshua who moved and destroyed without question. The violation of another people's sovereignty wasn't even questioned. Pretender god Jehovah ordained it, and the highly conditioned Israelites marched forward in their mission of slaughter.

These devastating sessions took a peace-loving people and conditioned them to do mighty battle. In this area, and others, the pretender gods began the conditioning. However, thanks to the major conditioning in the desert and the implementation of religion that was also part of humanity's heritage, humans reached a point where they were able to condition themselves. With most of the pretender gods gone for 2,800 years, much of the human race still continues to condition itself to do the ancient bidding of its perverse pretender gods.

So many of our mythological and holy books point out that we at first resisted the conditioning. A good example of this is the Indian warrior Arjuna.

In the *Bhagavad Gita* and the *Mahabharata*, the warrior Arjuna wants to work out a peace with his "enemies." However, Krishna at first persuades and then eventually goads Arjuna into fighting. How amazing that very few people are willing to see Krishna as the warmonger and Arjuna as the willing peacemaker. Because Krishna is seen as a god, most who read this account figure that Krishna must have been right.

He wasn't.

He was a technologically advanced being who was more interested in overcoming boredom and conquering territory. He may have been interested in the spiritual development of Arjuna's soul, but that spiritual development came at an awesome price. Many other aspects of the life of Krishna point out that he was much more spiritually sound than Jehovah. However, with both Jehovah and Krishna, modern humans give into to their conditioned tendency to develop selective memory when it comes to the gods they worship.

One only needs to look as far as the *Old Testament* to see an example of a god meddling in the process of peacemaking. Moses and Pharaoh had worked out a separate peace, but Jehovah would have none of it. He wanted slaughter – and most likely he also wanted good theater:

> And the Lord said to Moses, "Go to the Pharaoh: For I have hardened his heart and the heart of his servants, that I might show my powers before him."
>
> Exodus 10:1

Meet Jehovah, the hardener of hearts.

What is so shocking in ancient and modern theology is that this "divine" meddling shocks very few theologians. A wrathful, vengeful "God" interceded between two men who had decided to make peace and insured that this "wartime theater" would continue on schedule. In no way was the desert warfare series going to be canceled. This, of course, led to the Red Sea slaughter that, according to one of David's Psalms, killed many on both sides.

Yet Moses and Pharaoh had worked it out. They had negotiated and come to a separate peace. But you don't dare negotiate a separate peace apart from warmonger Jehovah (or any other of the pretender gods). Jehovah wanted blood, and would have none of these human or humane qualities interfering with his "ordained" plan. Jehovah needed to get his Israelites out into the desert so that he could whip them into shape and make damn sure that no peacemakers ever messed with his plans again.

This was not a one-time occurrence. The same "march in the desert" group was now under the "leadership" of Joshua. Once again, one of the cities wanted to work things out peacefully with Joshua:

> All of the cities did not attempt to make peace with the children of Israel, with the exception of the Hivites, who lived in Gibeon. Everyone else fought in battle.
>
> But the Lord hardened their hearts so that they would battle with Israel, that Israel might destroy them completely, and that they would find no fortune, but that Israel might destroy them.
>
> Joshua 11: 19-20

What a joyful piece of scripture! This reveals that peacemakers were spurned, and then conditioned to fight a battle they didn't want to fight.

Who is this hardener of hearts? Not the true God because the true God would never harden anyone's heart. The true God would be the creator of peace. However, this "God" of the Israelites wanted the taste of blood... as long as it wasn't his own.

The Modern Fallout of Ancient Conditioning

This is spiritual rape. The conditioning has etched itself so deeply into our cellular memory that slaughtering by the Serbs in Bosnia and the slaughter by both sides in Rwanda seems more like a natural reflex that a horrific act.

The holocaust of 6,000,000 Jews was an easy process. True, we cringe in horror after it happened, but during the actual holocaust, the Christians smelled the bodies burning and could sense that hundreds of human bodies were being burned each day close to their neighborhoods. However, they could not or would not resist. This comes as much from war conditioning as slave conditioning. Deep inside cellular memory plays a slave chip that shouts, "This is ordained from a higher power and resistance will not be tolerated."

These pretender gods conditioned us well. These "wonderful" pretender gods beat us into submission if we dared to move out of our "slave chip" paradigm.

Five thousand years later a group of prisoners in the Second World War Polish concentration camp in Sobibor decided they had had enough and planned an escape for all six hundred members. Ukrainian soldiers and Polish Jewish citizens (people who had been conditioned for years to distrust each other) worked together to bring about the only successful mass escape from a World War II concentration camp.

However, when this escape began, some couldn't move. Even with most of the SS officers already killed, many simply could not run to their freedom. They simply stood with heads bowed and prayed instead of running for freedom. That's powerful conditioning – conditioning which began thousands of years ago and continues today like a slave chip playing in our collective brains.

What could the pretender gods do to us then that caused us to be like that today?

CHAPTER SIX

Jehovah's Devastating Covenant –
An Offer We Couldn't Refuse

Anyone reading Jehovah's words of the Covenant that "He" made with his people would put most people in a state of shock. Fortunately, in most Christian and Jewish circles, the words of this highly oppressive document are neither read nor discussed. Outside of the context of the *Old Testament*, one would have to conclude that these were either the words of a raving lunatic or the ramblings of someone no longer grounded in reality.

However, this devastating document begins quite peacefully.

> If you follow my laws and faithfully observe
> my commandments,
> I will grant you rains in their season so that
> the earth shall yield its produce and the trees
> of the field their fruit.
> Your threshing shall overtake the vintage,
> and the vintage shall overtake the sowing;
> you shall eat your fill of bread and dwell
> securely in your land.
> I will grant peace in the land, and you will
> lie down untroubled by anyone; I will give
> the land respite from vicious beasts, and no
> sword shall cross your land.
> You shall give chase to your enemies, and
> they shall fall before you by the sword...
> I will look with favor upon you, and make
> you fertile and multiply you; and I will
> maintain my covenant with you.
> You shall eat grain long stored...
>
> Leviticus 26:3-10

Thus begins the words of Jehovah to the Israelites. Sounds like a fair deal... right? Think for a moment about this. Consider for a moment that you own a thriving business; you are doing quite well with your own business initiative. In comes a well-dressed character and says, "I have a deal for you. If you will pay me $3,000 a month, I will make sure that your business continues to be successful."

You mention that your business is doing quite well on its own. You don't need help from anyone.

Then the man leans closer to you and says, "You don't understand. If you don't pay us the $3,000 each month, we're going to stand outside your door and tell people that we've been cheated. We're going to tell people that you won't honor your commitments and that your merchandise will break down within weeks. We're going to tell people that you're planning to go out of business within weeks and that your customers will be stuck with your product."

You laugh that off. Now, the ones making the offer explain that they will create so many fires in your store that you will no longer be able to get the insurance you need to insure your remaining in business.

Immediately, you recognize the protection racket. These people are simply protecting you from the wrath that they intend to wreak upon you. You are gaining nothing, but you still have to pay for things to remain the same. You realize that these people have the power to accomplish what they promised, and this concerns you.

What does this have to do with Jehovah? Read on:

> But if you do not obey me and do not observe these commandments,
>
> If you reject my laws and spurn my norms, so that you do not observe all of my commandments and you break my Covenant, I in turn will do this to you. I will wreak misery upon you – consumption and fever, which cause the eyes to pine and the body to languish; you shall sow your seed to no purpose, for your enemies shall eat it.
>
> I will set my face against you; you shall be routed by your enemies, and your foes shall dominate you. You shall flee though none pursues.

Leviticus 26:14-17

This is not a loving God who cares for his children. This is instead a highly manipulative warlord claiming to be God – a pretender to the throne. This is a petty entity incapable of gentle persuasion who is spiritually raping the people he claims to love.

Hang on, it gets "better":

> And if for all that you do not obey me, I
> will go on disciplining you sevenfold for
> your sins, and I will break your proud glory.
> I will makethe skies like iron and your earth
> like copper, so that your strength shall be
> spent to no purpose.
> Your land shall not yield its produce, nor
> shall the trees of it yield their fruit.
>
> Leviticus 26:18-20

Sevenfold for your sins? Isn't this a bit excessive, Mr. Jehovah? What happened to an eye for an eye? This is seven days of detention for an offense requiring one day. This is swatting a dog on seven different occasions for defecating *once* on the rug.

Plainly, this is cruel and unusual punishment – the kind of punishment meted out by vengeful people set on effecting a vendetta. Yet few – even in the mob – would mete out a seven-fold vendetta.

Instead, this is the pronouncement of a very sick mind. Yet Jehovah told the Israelites that he was God – the only God worthy of being worshipped. By his very actions this pretender god was worthy of nothing but our contempt.

However, in this "deal" which Jehovah is forcing on his people, it gets even worse:

> And if for all that, you do not obey me, I
> will go on disciplining you seven-fold for
> your sins. I will loose wild beasts against
> you, and they shall bereave you of your chil-
> dren, and wipe out your cattle....
> ...and if you withdraw into your cities, I will
> send pestilence among you, and you shall
> be delivered into enemy hands.... You shall
> eat the flesh of your sons and the flesh of
> your daughters.... I will heap your carcasses
> on your lifeless fetishes.
> I will spurn you. I will lay your cities in
> ruin and make your sanctuaries desolate....

> And you will scatter among nations, and I
> will unsheathe the sword against you. Your
> land shall become a desolation and your cit-
> ies a ruin.
>
> Leviticus 26:21-33

What a guy! Is this the loving father who sent his only-begotten son into the world to save collective humanity from sin? Isn't this just a bit inconsistent? As mentioned before, maybe Jesus was adopted. How can a "God" who claimed that disobedient people would be reduced to eating the flesh and blood of their sons and daughters be resolved with the God who sent his only begotten son to save the world from sin?

Christian O'Brien, author of *The Genius of the Few*, claims that this covenant was disturbing for four reasons:

1) It was not a freely negotiated agreement between both parties.
2) The punishments proposed weren't even close to being civilized.
3) People other than the offenders would be punished – the good would have to suffer along with the bad.
4) Sin was being returned with evil – the punishment went far beyond the elements of the "crime."

However, understanding the dark side of Jehovah is essential. This is the entity that ordered a man stoned to death for picking up sticks on the Sabbath (Numbers 15:32-36). This is the entity who threw poisonous snakes into a crowd of people – and killed many of them – simply because they were complaining (Numbers, Chapter 21). This is the entity that beamed with joy when he was told by one of his followers that another follower had impaled someone because he was not obeying the commandments. This same entity beamed with joy when one of his followers ran a spear through a man and a woman. The man's crime was sex with an outsider. (Numbers 25)

This is also the entity – which despite claiming to be omnipotent – warned only seven people of an impending natural disaster and watched from above as millions of his creations died a terrifying death by drowning. Even those who were saved couldn't have been that impressed because they were all numbed by self-induced drunkenness within a few days – and nothing in the account indicates that the surviving seven were drinking to celebrate. This is the entity that a majority of Americans worship as the God of the Christians and the Jews.

This is also the "God" who spiritually raped us – his new creations – and created the past shock that lies deep within each and every one of us. This is the entity who insured that we would continue to worship him long after he departed – leaving us to our own resources and what writer Julian Jaynes claims were thousands of years of collective psychosis.

Exactly how did these pretender gods do that? He and his cohorts created a highly effective system of conditioning that was so effective that its devastating impact has remained thousands of years after their departure. What these pretender gods gave us to keep us in line was religion.

CHAPTER SEVEN

The Origins of Religion: Conditioning the New Creations to Be Spiritual Slaves

For much of this chapter, I would like you to assume a different perspective. While you are most familiar with the human experience, move your perspective to a different level. For now, assume that you are very high up in the ranks of these pretender gods. You created the human race as a slave race – a herd of worker humans to do your dirty work. Thanks to the hordes of newly created humans toiling for you, you now have more leisure time. Eventually, you decide that you need some warriors to help you conquer lands from the other entities that were mining the planet.

This different viewing point will attempt to explain what caused a very rebellious humanity to become much more obedient. To use a related analogy, we know the murderers and we have millions of dead bodies. The sacred and mythological writings give war after war to explain this proliferation of slaughter. However, explaining how all of this carnage became linked to holiness and God will be a little bit harder. Because the pretender gods often controlled the writing of many of the holy books, the move toward creating religion would understandably have been censored or disguised.

What we do know is that the pretender gods increasingly became bored. They needed something that would take the edge off their arduous work. Now that the newly created humans had lightened their workload, the pretender gods needed something to occupy their increased amounts of free time. At first, this was war and battle. Later, especially between battles and during the lulls of peace, the pretender gods needed something to keep themselves interested.

During the battles, the human warriors were in increasing numbers refusing to fight. Other workers in the mines and in other menial jobs are refusing to work. Some of the humans were beginning to riot. And – God forbid – many, when they realized that their lives didn't show much promise, were now committing suicide.

This was happening during a time long after the final genetic experiments had been finalized. While the human race was far more obedient and compliant than the original creations, problems were beginning to crop up, and these problems were increasing.

Needed: A Control Mechanism

Just how do you make sure that your relatively new creations fight your wars, do your dirty work, and stop committing suicide? After much discussion at the highest levels, the pretender gods must have finally discovered an answer – create a religion.

With this religion you would promise rewards in the next life. You would mention that this would be for eternity. To gain this eternal life, your creations would have to play your game, your way, for the rest of their lives. This means sweating and toiling without rebellion. This would also include worshipping those who created you. For those of your new creations who are unimpressed, you invent a place called Hell.

Hell promises great misery for eternity – misery much worse than anything experienced on Earth now. To insure that your rebellious charges continue fighting your wars, you promise that dying in war is an automatic ticket to a much better place: Heaven, Paradise, Avalon. Of course, as the creators of all this, you get to pick and choose who goes where.

As self–ascended gods, you boldly assert that those who are thinking about committing suicide will automatically go to hell and suffer torment for eternity. This insures that those humans who get depressed with their woeful present conditions will remain with those woeful conditions, stuck fast in the hope that they will eventually get to rest for eternity. To insure that they will spend eternity in heaven, these effectively conditioned and spiritually raped humans will spend their free time worshipping their creators, bending to their every whim.

Because the pretender gods have successfully blocked any memory of the human's concept of their own spirit – and blocked all memory of past lives – the humans have no way to determine whether this is real or false. Since this religion is a game for eternity, most of the humans quickly realize that it is best to play the game of the pretender gods. At this time in history, it's the only game in town.

The Cosmic "Good Cop/Bad Cop" Routine

Being one of these pretender gods, you had to be totally sure that your creations played your game according to your rules. To insure that this happened, you create a cosmic "good cop/bad cop" routine. This is the embodiment of a force which is trying to keep you in a state of sin (wanting to worship other gods, not obeying the dictates of the gods, not wanting to work, lusting after other women without intention of procreation, etc.). You claim that this other entity wants your soul, and if this entity succeeds, you will spend all of eternity in hell.

If this newly created entity wins, you lose. Problem is that your life will be a lot more fun and work a lot better if this entity wins. It's all very confusing.

Being exploited by these pretender gods, the humans begin to believe that this is the evil one working in their lives. You tell the humans that they should pray to be guided by the forces of righteousness... which are of course you. The same response is generated when anyone wants to make peace with your enemies instead of simply killing them in battle.

When any of the humans' rebellious forces experience spasms of awareness about what is being done to them, you can condition them into believing that those who promise liberation are evil. This is what happened with the serpent in the Garden of Eden. This is what happened with Prometheus when he stole fire from the gods and gave it to humanity. This is also what happened with the Norse god Loki who threw a monkey wrench into the slave conditioning of the gods and made things so unbearable for them that they finally had to leave.

Until the Thirteenth Century, the Norse God Loki was considered to be a liberator. However, as the European countries became Christianized, Loki was eventually considered to be Satan. Other pagan gods suffered the same fate, as dualistic religion began to take hold in the Northern European Countries.

To insure that this dualistic conditioning remained firm, you invent some chants which instill and deepen the conditioning:

We are evil and deserve our lot.

Working for the Lord is wonderful.

I will die in battle for the Lord.

In hymns like "Onward Christian Soldiers" the fruits of this conditioning linger on. The music is rousing, and I sang it joyfully as a young adult. However, like so many others of the human race, I willingly continued the ancient brainwashing and insured that my slave chip remained intact.

The musically magnificent "Amazing Grace" contains lines like "Amazing grace, that saved a wretch like me." We continue our slave chip conditioning and add another stick to the fires of internal hell by conditioning our brains to believe that we are not worthy of the true God, the One who created our souls.

Our Programmed Need to Worship

The true God knows that we are worthy and does not demand that we constantly prove ourselves. He [she/it] does not demand conditioning or slavery. And this true God certainly does not demand religion. This true God is a force that offers freedom and invites all sentient beings to tap into "His" power and break free of all past conditioning and lies.

Because of past shock, this is not an easy task. The pretender gods stepped into our lives claiming to be the true God. Because the true God is a force, it was very easy to accept that these technologically superior gods must indeed be God.

This happened in World War II in New Guinea with the Cargo Cult. The indigenous natives saw planes flying in and unloading supplies at the air bases. These natives believed that these planes must be gods because they had never seen anything like this before. Therefore, they began worshipping the planes as gods.

When the war ended and the planes stopped coming in, the natives built replicas of planes to lure these "gods" back. Twenty years after the end of the war, natives were still sitting in expectation for a big god/plane to come down from the sky and land.

I remember seeing this example displayed in the 1963 Italian film *Mondo Cane*. It is the last scene in this documentary film, and the pictures of natives staring at the sky in vain hopes for a plane returning is a very powerful image. My date for this film was a devout Catholic woman who emphatically stated how pathetic the natives were for not realizing that the plane wasn't going to come. Within fifteen minutes, she was talking about how she expected Jesus to return in this decade.

What she did not realize was that all of Jesus' disciples had expected Jesus to return rather quickly after his death and alleged resurrection. The book of "Revelations" ends with the Greek expression, "Maranatha, Kyrios" (Come soon, Lord). Yet the disciples, those highly revered saints whom we venerate, died not seeing their Lord return, despite the fact that Jesus promised that he would return before they died.

A strangely devoted group of people grew up around this expectation. Pillar saints were people who were so sure that Jesus was going to return in the first or second century that they sat atop pillars hoping they could get the first glance of Jesus returning. The devotion may have been something to be admired. However, their efforts were futile.

Let's not be too hard on Jesus. A student of religious history will quickly discover accounts of sixteen other crucified and resurrected saviors (Virishna, Mithras, Viracocha, etc.). What all of these sixteen – and

Jesus – promised is that they would return. What all seventeen have in common is that they have not returned. Since some of these crucified and resurrected saviors go back more than 5,000 years, this is not a good record. It causes one to wonder if Jesus will actually return as he promised.

Yet, in 1963 when millions of people saw *Mondo Cane*, a collective superiority complex must have been generated as viewers watched these "pathetic" natives looking to the sky in expectation of the return of their god/plane.

Are we really any better off by hoping that Jesus is going to return? Could we instead be suffering from the fallout of past shock? Could we feel such a sense of abandonment that we want those who raped our souls to return and do it again? Are we really reflecting a sane wish when we want to return to that ancient version of "that old time religion?"

Conditioning Away the Divine Spark

Only the false pretender gods would have created religions. For the most part, religions do not liberate. They have too much baggage from the past to do that. Religions set themselves up to be dominated by a "priest class." This ruling priest class eventually turns out to be far more concerned with domination and spiritual slavery than the spiritual freedom that is everyone's birthright.

This happened after the pretender gods departed, and it is happening now.

The newly formed human race must have sensed this desire to dominate. They must have sensed that those who claimed to be God simply could not be God. Deep within was the divine spark of freedom, and the emerging humans most likely wanted to fan this spark into a flame. However, the pretender gods simply could not let this happen. Allowing this spiritual freedom would have destroyed the pretender gods' original intentions – having a worker class of beings to do their dirty work.

To insure that humans would work and later fight, the pretender gods eventually created religion as a way to insure that humans would not discover the true God. By usurping the role of the true God and backing this up with their superior technology, they raped our innocence and inflicted upon us the false concept of original sin. This helped keep us ensnared in guilt.

The *Old Testament* and other apocryphal books are full of Jehovah's obsessive ramblings. He berated the innocent by making up sins and then inflicted severe punishment upon those who dared to stray from his "divinely ordained" path.

To compound this horrific past shock, Jehovah and the other pretender gods created religion as a way to keep this emerging race of humans in line. Worship was meant to keep humans in a state of awe about the pretender gods. Those who didn't worship were in trouble. Those who dared to lack a sense of awe were either ostracized or punished brutally.

(Neil Freer in his book *Breaking the Godspell* speaks of this past shock as a "godspell" – a spell woven upon unsuspecting humans to keep them conditioned to worship. Freer also points out the great irony that the word "worship" in ancient times meant "to work for.")

Hellish Conditioning

In the name of religion, wars were fought. The pretender gods found a way to condition humans to believe that killing other people in the name of the Lord was somehow spiritual. Those who died in battle were seen as heroes instead of pathetically conditioned fighters. Jehovah's forty-year wilderness trek was a highly conditioned boot camp in which some peace-loving humans were effectively conditioned into being war machines.

Those with human qualities were eventually seen as "yellow" and not wanting to fulfill one's duty of fighting for the Lord. This horrendous conditioning still continues on today, as some radical Islamic fundamentalists see America as the Great Satan and have visions of eventually destroying this "force of evil." This conditioning was so powerful that two Islamic nations – Iraq and Iran – fought each other for eight years before ending their highly destructive war with no winner. This was like two pit bulls ripping each other almost to death, and for what outcome?

Lest we as Americans feel that we are superior to this conditioning, within months we were bashing the infidel Arabs in the Gulf War. There, we killed innocent people with little or no compassion. We deluded ourselves into believing that smart bombs were only killing military people. This pathetic conditioning is worldwide, and if not put in check will eventually destroy us as a species.

The pretender gods did their work well.

They created holy days, and then provided absurd instruction about what one could do and not do during these holy days. As mentioned before, the *Old Testament* tells of a man who was stoned to death because he dared to pick up a stick on the Sabbath day.

In the Name of God, Thou Shalt Not Search for God

All of this was done in the name of God. The true God got buried under the weight of this conditioning. In one of the cruelest ironies in human history, the search for the true God became the ultimate sin. Thanks to our ancient religious conditioning, many of us still continue to feel guilty if we feel the urgings of the true God. As this true God urges us to break free of this awful conditioning, conditioned voices come forth in our mind screaming, "You are straying from the sacred path!" This religious conditioning helps us to feel that we will go to hell if we dare break free of the pretender gods' conditioning.

What a cruel irony: if we break free of what is creating a hell on Earth, many "instinctively" feel that they will go to hell for eternity. As a result, so many of us continue to enslave ourselves in the name of God.

As a young boy I experienced this conditioning in the form of well meaning neighbors who told me that God wanted me to read the Bible every day. If I didn't, I was yielding to the urgings of the devil and endangering my mortal soul. When I dared ask in Sunday school why God would strike a man dead for trying to save the Ark of the Covenant, my Sunday school teacher surrendered to her conditioning by telling me that God in his wisdom knew what he was doing. It was not appropriate for us as humans to question "His" motives.

I was often reminded that God was an angry God who would punish and test us mightily to keep us in line. Ironically, my father – fearing that I was going too far in my teenage zealousness – used punishment as a means to "save me from salvation." However, my conditioning was powerful. At that time, I only saw him as an instrument of the devil trying to keep me from going to Saturday night Youth for Christ rallies. In his own way, he was trying to keep me from one form of conditioning. However, he insisted that I go to Sunday school and church at the family church – another form of conditioning.

We will never break free of the shackles of religious conditioning as long as we remain stuck in the mentality that one form of religious conditioning is better than someone else's.

Conditioning is conditioning.

It blocks the spiritual freedom that the true God gave every human soul. Conditioning a child to believe in a certain way merely continues the devastating conditioning which was inflicted upon us thousands of years ago.

Pretender God Religion: Insuring the Soul against God

The creation of religion has had a devastating impact on the human soul. It instills fear and stultifies spiritual exploration. People who doubt their conditioned god are seen as backsliders who are "steeped in sin." Those who explore alternatives to this conditioning are seen as heretics. Those who break free of this conditioning are seen as blasphemers. Those wanting to break free fear are seen by some as damning their souls for eternity.

Not only did the creation of religion create a devastating impact upon the human soul, but also the acts of history itself continued this impact. Many still continue to think that the Crusades were a wonderful Christian event.

It may have been Christian, but it wasn't wonderful.

Not being satiated from their slaughter of Islamic infidels, these "knights for Christ" looted and burned Christian villages. Whether Islamic or Christian, the people they conquered were brutally treated. The women were raped – often after they were dead. Babies were roasted over an open fire, and these "Knights for Christ" sang hymns of thanks for finally getting to eat some meat. Accounts from diaries tell of pouring molten lead on the faces of screaming babies. The more humane of these knights did offer a chance to convert to Christianity before killing their victims.

During the Spanish Inquisition, humans inflicted a wonderful form of conditioning upon other humans. Those lacking the spiritually correct cluster of beliefs were roasted in the town square. John Hus, a Czech reformer, merely wanted to have the Bible translated into Czech so that the people could read the Bible for themselves. He also made the bold assertion that Jesus was the head of the Christian Church and not Rome.

This so enraged the ruling priest class that Hus and thousands of his followers were burned at the stake in the main square of Constance during the Council of Constance. The main reason for this six-year Council was to determine which of three people claiming to be pope was really pope. If one of these "popes" hadn't died right before the Council, the deliberations might have taken much longer. One of the other popes, realizing that he had fallen out of favor with the Council members, sneaked out of town. Leaving only one pope fighting for legitimacy didn't appear to speed things up.

This might have been because the Council of Constance had a few sideshows to keep things interesting. John Hus and Jerome of Prague were being tried for heresy.

This Council, like so many of the other Councils of Christian history, felt compelled to determine which beliefs were spiritually correct. During all of this there wasn't a pretender god in sight. They had been gone for nearly 2,200 years. Yet, their ancient conditioning was still rearing its ugly head. The creation of religion was still extracting a devastating price.

Both John Hus and Jerome of Prague were not going against the Bible. They simply wanted to allow the Bible to be translated in the language of the Czech people. Neither claimed that Jesus was no longer the head of the church. In fact, they wanted to restore Jesus as the head of the church.

John Hus had been promised safe passage by Emperor Sigusmond if he would come to the Council of Constance and present his views. Upon arrival, he was immediately arrested. Both were burned at the stake after long periods of time rotting in disease infested prisons.

These are the fruits of a religion that has lost its soul and run out of control. The pretender gods may have departed, but its devastating fall-out remains.

Would these pretender gods have been proud of this? Or would they have recoiled in horror to see what had happened to their creations? Could they have seen that their conditioning from the creation of religion would help create the World War II Holocaust and the present horrors in Bosnia? Here, the gang-raping of Islamic women would simply be seen as the spoils of war. Would the pretender gods have gasped in disbelief if they knew how difficult creating and maintaining a peace would be between the Israeli's and the Palestinians?

The Song Is Over, but the Melody Lingers On

These pretender gods might have left, but their conditioning remains. Inside each and every one of us is a slave chip that continues the conditioning of the pretender gods. This slave chip is the result of many genetic experiments and thousands of years of religious conditioning. We play out this conditioning today as if the pretender gods were still in our midst. The singer of the song might be gone, but the melody lingers on with a devastating impact.

A true story is told of a soldier during the Korean War who was told to guard a certain area until he was relieved. What he did not realize is that his squad was quietly wiped out by the enemy. Thus, for three days he continued to guard the area. Finally, into the fourth day he collapsed from exhaustion. When he woke up, he felt tremendous guilt because he had fallen asleep. He had no way of knowing that no one could possibly relieve him. So he continued in his guilt, sensing that it was his fault that his squadron had been wiped out. Somehow, he was able to generate in his mind that if he had stayed awake, he might have been able to save his troops.

He was not guilty, but thanks to a convoluted conditioning, he ended up feeling very guilty. He continues to carry that guilt with him today more than forty years later.

Humanity is collectively like that soldier. As early humans, we were conditioned to worship interlopers and pretenders as God. These pretenders deserted us and left us to our own resources to survive because they no longer had need of us or Earth's resources. That awesome and devastating conditioning remains with us. Like sheep, many continue the patterns of worship. Many still offer their bodies to fight the "holy" wars – and have hopes of paradise for participating in the slaughter.

Our world of work still is not structured to serve the worker. Instead god-like "superiors" are paid much more than they are worth because they can easily find worker drones that will work for much less than they are worth.

We are so well conditioned that almost any movement toward spiritual liberation will create guilt and a feeling that one is falling from the fold. We have been programmed well. We tend to feel spiritually nourished to the degree that we remain spiritual slaves.

With no guidance from the pretender gods – or God himself – religious zealots burned John Hus at the stake. Well meaning "men of God" threatened Galileo with brutal torture, and forced him to recant what we know today is true. Representatives of God captured American hostages from the embassy of "The Great Satan" in the late 1970's. Godly people slaughtered whole cities in the name of Christ, raped and slaughtered the Indians they were trying to convert, and held heresy trails and painful executions for those who dared not believe.

Worshipping the Spiritual Rapists

Too many continue to praise a long-gone group of pretender gods "which saved a wretch like me." Too many of us continue to see ourselves as sin-bound creatures. Those who "refuse" to see themselves as sin-bound still suffer from the dumbing down of the pretender gods. We walk this planet with a brain that is capable of moving mountains, yet we continue to stumble over anthills.

In one of history's most cosmic ironies, many continue to glorify and sing hymns to the very entities that molested our free will and raped our spiritual sovereignty.

We are victims of a long past spiritual rape that has made past shock a part of our experience. The more we are willing to face what actually happened in the past, the more we will be able to overcome this past shock and begin living as the humans that we are capable of becoming.

This means that we will have to look at our religions with a new vision. We will have to be bold and explore exactly why religions were created in the first place. This is an exciting time. New discoveries in archeological digs are providing written material that will add to our data banks of understanding.

This began in the late 1940's with the discovery of the Dead Sea Scrolls and the Nag Hamadi Library.

While many claim that all the Dead Sea Scrolls have been translated and published, many researchers do not share this opinion. Michael Baigent and Richard Leigh in *The Dead Sea Scrolls Deception* claim that at least three books are locked up in the Vatican basement. Their material is so controversial that church authorities don't want this material released. The church fathers do not want people to know what was contained in three epistles written by James the Just (the brother of Jesus). James thought that the newly converted apostle Paul was not yet ready to go out and preach. James referred to Paul as the Great Liar and the Instrument of Satan. Considering that the words of Paul take up more than four times the space as the words of Jesus, one could understand why such a discovery would rattle the foundations of Christianity.

Paul 4, Jesus 1

Following their conditioning well and making sure that spiritual manipulation would continue, the church fathers opted to place the words of Paul as the main force in the *New Testament*. I was told during my seminary instruction that this was ordained by the Holy Spirit, and Paul's words should be considered the word of God. When I asked why God didn't just send Paul out instead of Jesus, I would get these strange looks.

Paul's words, despite some magnificent passages on spiritual freedom, lean more toward insuring that people remain obedient.

The words of Jesus Christ are more oriented toward spiritual liberation.

One can understand why the church fathers felt they needed to place the words of Paul in the *New Testament* in a four to one ratio to the words of Jesus. One can further understand why further parts of the Dead Sea Scrolls are never going to be released to the public. The Dead Sea Scrolls, once understood, will probably contribute more to spiritual freedom than spiritual slavery.

Discoveries like these come as the result of great searching. Those who simply allow their priest, minister, or rabbi to spiritually guide them will not discover these realities. Granted, most of these spiritual leaders do mean well. However, they simply are not aware of what is being discovered on an almost daily basis.

The ultimate discovery will be humanity's collective increasing awareness why religions were created in the first place.

This will take great courage and a desire to explore rather than submit.

The exploration has already begun.

The time to intensify this exploration is now.

CHAPTER EIGHT

The Devastating Impact of
Ancient Religion on the Human Soul

The pretender gods programmed the new humans well. Humans were collectively convinced that they were nothing without their "gods." Demanding worship and obedience, the pretender gods failed to instill a sense of self-worth in their creations. Instead, the work they did, how well they fought in battle, and how much they revered the pretender gods determined their value.

What the pretender gods originally got was a human species with great mental and spiritual potential. Sadly, these humans were not allowed to use this accident of creation. If Zecharia Sitchin is right in saying that humans at least 10,000 years ago were capable of building rocket ships, the dumbing down which followed was devastating. If Adam and Eve were able to see clearly like the pretender gods, the residue of that ensuing dumbing down made a formidable impact on humans then.

That impact continues today. If humans had godlike powers when they were building the Tower of Babel, we certainly have descended far from that potential.

Rather than being the creators they were capable of being, the emerging humans were often relegated to the task of being food-preparers for the gods:

> Speak unto the children of Israel and say
> unto them, "When you come into the land
> of your habitations which I give unto you,
> And will make an offering unto the Lord, a
> burnt offering, or a sacrifice in performing
> a vow, or in a freewill offering, or in your
> solemn feasts to make a sweet savor unto
> the Lord, of the herd, or of the flock...."
>
> Numbers 15: 2-3

The ultra-lazy Jehovah is setting up a potluck for himself and his cohorts. This is done in the name of "making a sacrifice unto the Lord." No one had the courage to say, "Hey, Jehovah, go out and prepare your own dinner." To be sure, many had said exactly this and ended up being stoned to death, having poisonous snakes thrown in their midst, or other forms of punishment ending in painful and humiliating death.

For the sake of needing to find a work force, we as humans were created. To insure that we would continue doing menial work instead of pursuing more scientific and creative pursuits, we were dumbed down. To insure that we would be effectively programmed to work hard and fight wars, we were given religion.

Dissent Within the Pretender God Ranks

Some of the humans' creators were not totally comfortable in the role of pretender gods. Some must have felt a great shame in programming their newly created humans to believe that they represented the true God. William Bramley in *The Gods of Eden* mentions how a group of pretender god dissenters tried to help the emerging humans by telling them the truth about the humans' spiritual nature.

The group was a disciplined brotherhood dedicated to the dissemination of spiritual knowledge and the attainment of spiritual freedom. Bramley refers to this group as "The Brotherhood of the Snake." Its members opposed the enslavement of spiritual beings, and according to the Egyptian writings, it sought to eliminate the human race from pretender god bondage. The "Brotherhood of the Snake" evidently imparted scientific knowledge and encouraged the high aesthetics that existed in many ancient societies.

However, the majority of the pretender gods wanted hard-working slaves. In addition, they wanted humans to worship and venerate them. As dumbed-down as some of the humans were, they still weren't buying that these pretenders were god. They needed a form of conditioning that would be so powerful that the humans themselves would willingly inflict it upon their children. That conditioning eventually evolved into organized religion.

At first, the pretender gods simply told their human charges that they were God. According to sacred and mythological writings, it didn't take long for the humans to figure out that the pretender gods weren't telling them the truth. Something stirring deep within them told them that they (the humans) were at least as spiritual, or perhaps even more spiritual, than the pretender gods. For a while, they were helped by those within the ranks of the pretender gods. These dissenters wanted to liberate humans from their slavery and help them discover their true spiritual nature; however, they were a minority, and the majority of the pretender gods offered good reasons for keeping the humans enslaved – both physically and spiritually:

> The Custodians [pretender gods] clearly did not want mankind to begin traveling the road to spiritual recovery. The reason is obvious. The Custodial society wanted slaves. It is difficult to make thralls of people who maintain their integrity and sense of ethics. It becomes impossible when these same individuals are uncowed by physical threats due to a reawakened grasp of their spiritual immortality. Most importantly, if spiritual beings could no longer be trapped in human bodies, but could instead use and abandon bodies at will, there would not be spiritual beings available to animate slave bodies.
>
> William Bramley, *The Gods of Eden*

The hearts of the members of the Brotherhood of the Snake were good. However, they eventually failed because the majority of the pretender gods wanted humans to remain as slave labor. They also wanted to be worshipped and revered. This is understandable – perhaps even human. However, it raped the souls of humanity as an emerging species.

The religion that the pretender gods created was very convenient. Humans were programmed to believe that any desire to be free was evil. They were told that those in the pretender gods' ranks who wanted to free them were misguided and malicious. In the name of religion – and holiness! – this programming was never-ending. We became like the savagely beaten dog that snarls at the stranger who is trying to set it free.

I am sure that a conversation like what follows must have occurred millions of times. The confused human has feelings deep within him – feelings that are burning to be expressed. In a cosmic "good cop/ bad cop" conditioning session, the "good cop" puts his arm around the confused human and walks with him:

> We understand that you are getting these strong feelings, but these feelings come from the evil one. The evil one is trying to convince you that you don't want to work. That's always what the evil one does when he wants to trap you and steal your soul. But God wants you to work hard, and we are giving you this wonderful opportunity.

> If you work hard in this life, you will get to rest for all of eternity.

Now the "master programmer" begins moving in for the kill:

> But you must be aware that there is a way that you could lose this chance for eternal rest very quickly. Even *listening* to the evil one could put your soul in danger. Even thinking that you are something other than a being that works gladly for us and worships us could cause you to suffer for eternity.

A final warning is issued, and a way out is suggested:

> You must not listen to those feelings inside of you. They are being generated by the evil one. Listen to us. We will tell you what the truth is because we are the True Gods.

The human is confused. Deep within him he senses a spark of his own divinity. Yet, he knows if he expresses it, he will incur the wrath of the pretender gods. However, this spark is beginning to fan itself into a flame. He discusses it with a trusted friend:

> I am very confused. These entities that claim to be God do not act the way I think God would. They want us to fight in wars; we want to make peace. They want us to be slaves; we want to be free. Something is wrong.

The trusted friend is further along with his programming. He had these feelings at one time until the pretender gods "set him straight."

> You are listening to the voice of evil. The wars we are fighting and the work we are doing is a wonderful opportunity to serve God. To think anything else is evil. We must worship them. We must do their prescribed rituals. And we must make sacrifices to them because they are our creators. We must honor them. To do anything less would be blasphemy.

The one giving the "sage" advice has two little children – a boy and a girl. He hopes that when his daughter comes to a ripe age that she will be chosen to be a "priestess" for the pretender gods. What an honor this would be. He hopes the son will become a hard and diligent worker – a worker who will bring honor to the family. When the boy is growing up, he will be told that Jehovah (Enlil, Zeus, Wotan) is the true God and deserves reverence and honor.

Many young boys and girls in those ancient times would get training from their parents about "the truth." Following the conditioning of the pretender gods, the mother and father will make sure that their children will be discouraged from thinking for themselves. In those moments that these young children dare to think for themselves, the parents will feel an obligation to set them straight:

> I had many of those same thoughts when I was your age. I thought at one time that the gods were trying to exploit us. But I soon realized that working for the gods and fighting for them is an honor, an honor we shouldn't take lightly. I realized that the 'evil one' was trying to tell me that I was great or better than they were, which is not so. And with this realization, I came to know that the gods love us. They are giving us an opportunity to do their will. Their wisdom is far superior to ours. They know what is best for us. Son, do their bidding. Worship them with great reverence. Otherwise, the evil one will destroy you.

With rituals, sacrifices, and worship services, the pretender gods deepened their conditioning of the human race. With this conditioning, the once-rebelling humans now became allies to their oppressors. Religion was created in such a way that submission was equated with holiness. And its fallout has lasted through the ages.

The First Kapos – The Ruling Priest Class

During the Second World War during the holocaust, the Germans depended on a group of prisoners known as kapos. The kapo was Jewish and did the will of the Germans – often beating their fellow Jews into submission. For doing this they were given extra privileges and a larger ration of food.

A higher class of kapo was the "oberkapo," a person of higher rank who had more authority and gained even more privileges. Thousands of years ago the foundation for kapos and oberkapos was being formed as the ancient roots of religion were beginning to take hold. A group of humans were formed which would continue the religious conditioning of the pretender gods. They were so faithful to the pretender gods that they had humans sent to their deaths for daring to think that the pretender gods were not the true Gods.

These beings were eventually referred to as priests.

They were given great power because they did their job well. When the pretender gods finally left, the priests remained to "keep the faith." They claimed to be in touch with the pretender gods and passed down terrifying messages of woe to those who dared not believe. In so many ways the priests and prophets of the pretender gods inflicted a greater level of past shock than the pretender gods themselves:

> I have come back from the mountain where
> I have been in discourse with the mighty
> Enlil. He tells me that your hearts are full
> of evil – that your hearts are more filled with
> lust than for the desire to worship the Mighty
> One. He demands that three women be sac-
> rificed immediately. Who among you will
> offer up his daughter for Enlil's appease-
> ment?

How strong the conditioning raged on as thirty fathers raced forward with their daughters fighting for the privilege of having their daughters thrown into the smoldering volcano. The pretender gods were no longer around, but the members of the ruling priest class had total control. They decided what clothing would be worn on holy days. They declared holidays or increased the workload. They determined who was worthy of the gods and who was straying. They genuinely believed that they heard the voice of their departed gods – much in the same manner that people in the New Age movement today claim to channel the wisdom of etheric entities from beyond our realm.

While most of what is channeled today is harmless and at worst vapid, the past "channelings" of the departed gods were devastating and continued the terrors of past shock long after the departure of the gods. In one of the cruelest of human ironies, some members of the more conservative Christian sects are speaking out vehemently against the vapid channeling of various discarnate entities. They reserve a special hostility for those entities channeling new age spirituality. With a greater integrity, these "fierce condemners" would be greater served by looking at some of the ancient "channelings" which did much more harm.

In the name of religion, personal freedom, personal fulfillment, and personal spirituality were sacrificed. In the Egyptian society a flexibility of different modes of work existed, but even that became more rigid. Moving from job to job became very difficult. Productivity was the true god of the pretender gods.

Even the pharaohs were conned by the pretender gods. Told that they would eventually be set free after death to join the pretender gods, the pharaohs conscripted help to build pyramids, temples, and tombs so that the pharaoh's ride to heaven would be insured. All of this was done in the name of "God." Somehow millions of Egyptians were conned into believing that their pharaoh deserved the first crack at being able to be with the gods.

Ancient Conditioning Subduing the Whisperings of the Soul

The humans sensed long ago that they were spiritual beings in a human body. However, the creation of religion dimmed this awareness and focused more on the human body as being the total being. Through religion, humanity was led to believe that their bodies would be taken to the next life. The idea of preserving bodies made sense thousands of years ago.

The pretender gods must have been aware of many spiritual truths. However, they realized that their human creations would be very difficult to manipulate if they revealed any of these truths. By creating a very complex religion full of arcane symbols, intricate rituals, and often-senseless rules, the human race found itself overwhelmed with what they were assured was the truth.

Offering a lamb covered with flour and a bullock covered with flour and oil – along with wine to wash it down was simply seen as something sacred because their gods requested it. (Numbers 15: 5-11). Today, a spiritually free soul would see nothing sacred in this. Lazy pretender gods wanted someone to prepare dinner for them and couched all of this in the name of religion. What we had back then was history's first recorded "shake and bake."

However, in the name of religion, Joshua and his horde pillaged the city of Jericho. The one who helped bring this about was a prostitute named Rahab. This woman was betraying the very people she lived with because... well, you know... they were wicked. This was a prostitute. This was a woman who went around having carnal knowledge without

Egyptians pharaohs believed the pyramids would give them access to heaven.

producing any spawn-to-be-conditioned workers for the gods. She owned a house in the city, and she sneaked out to help Joshua and his religiously conditioned warriors learn about the city so that it could be efficiently and quickly destroyed.

The books of James and Hebrews in the *New Testament* praise Rahab for her faith. Yet Rehab was a traitor to her own people. She was the only one to live after the carnage of Jericho. Her motives must have been obvious even to Joshua. Yet in two books of the New Testament, she is held up as a paragon of faith.

As James Michener mentioned so astutely in *The Bridge at Andau*, prostitutes are opportunists. Days before the brutal October 1956 Russian attack on Budapest, prostitutes were observed leaving Hungary weeks, even months, before the event. Michener explained that prostitutes have a certain "knowing" (no pun intended). They pack up and leave well in advance of a military base's closing. Rahab knew that the wind was changing, and she wanted to be on the right side. Glorifying her betrayal either in the Old or the New Testaments misses the point.

However, in this battle, good ol' Jehovah might have had an even "holier" agenda.

> And they burnt the city with fire, and all
> that was therein: only the silver, and the
> gold, and the vessels of brass and iron, they
> put into the treasury of the house of the Lord.
>
> Joshua 6:24

Now I get it. Jehovah wanted to beef up his treasury. He wanted some more toys. And he conned the people doing his dirty work into believing that this had some holy significance. He drove that "holy" significance home by brutally slaughtering one man who dared to keep two pieces of gold for himself. This man forgot the eleventh commandment: "Though shalt not hoard even a shred of Jehovah's booty." Not only was this man brutally slaughtered, but his wife, children, and even his uncles, aunts, nieces, and nephews were also slaughtered. This was all done for hoarding two pieces of gold. But then again, he did do something that he was explicitly told not to do.

I guess Jehovah in his wisdom thought that this was best.

Jehovah appeared to respect gold and silver much more than the people of his chosen race.

Imagine a twelve-year old boy shot to death by a firing squad of his junior high school peers. His offense: mouthing off to the teacher. Now imagine that group of bloodthirsty boys and girls marching over to the offending boy's home and rousting out the boy's mother, father, and two sisters. All four are shot to death. After all, if the parents and siblings had been more responsible, the boy probably would not have had such bad manners. The law claims that other relatives must be speedily executed. A lone voice cries out for mercy and compassion. That voice is silenced with four well aimed shots.

This modern version obviously sounds quite absurd. Yet this is one of the most devastating aspects of past shock. Somehow when these atrocities are done in the past, they are more digestible. Perhaps some readers of this ridiculous modern example would feel better if the young man physically attacked his teacher instead of just verbally abusing her. Some might go as far as to claim that nothing should happen to the boy and his family unless the boy actually took a life.

But they would still need to execute the boy's family.

This admittedly absurd sense of justice points out the horror of Jehovah's "justice."

But whether in modern or ancient times, isn't this overdoing it just a bit? Isn't it time to question our religious conditioning and ask if such heinous acts are valid? Can we muster the courage to admit to ourselves that we have been religiously conned? Or will we continue the stranglehold of past shock by claiming that "God in his wisdom knew what he was doing, and it is not for us as mortal humans to question the Lord's actions."

Bull! We are spiritual beings who should know better. We boldly need to explore those writings which we erroneously insist are mythology. We should see what Jehovah really was – a "control freak," totally out of control. However, the presence of Jehovah and the other pretender gods reinforced their creation of ritual, ornamentation, priests, and religion. Jehovah conned humans into believing that something holy existed about the slaughter of people and the self-inflicted rape of the human soul.

The fact that most of what they were commanded to do broke most of the Ten Commandments is something missed by modern humanity.

Jehovah would have been happy to know that a group of misfits known as the Crusaders pillaged and plundered city after city in the name of his alleged son. Despite their original goal of freeing Jerusalem from the infidels, they attacked Christian and "infidel" enclaves and left a trail of slaughter and pillage in their wake.

Why? Because they had religious conditioning from long ago which convinced them that both the "infidel" and their Christian brothers were... well, wicked.

Past shock has not departed: it has only become more refined and acceptable.

Just twenty-one verses later after the "shake and bake" sacrifice recorded in Numbers 15 is one of the most horrifying event in the Old Testament: the old man who dared to gather sticks on the Sabbath. In the name of God, in the name of religion, that man was brutally stoned to death. Nothing at all godly exists in Jehovah's pronouncement that this be done. Jehovah was a pretender to the throne of God. He was mentally sick and physically vicious. And he is one of many who created many horrifying aspects of organized religion that continues to perpetuate this sickness today.

The failure of many religions to address and apologize for errors spawned out of their dark history has damaged the credibility of well-meaning religions.

At least the Greeks had many gods to worship. However, Jehovah boldly proclaimed that he was a jealous god and that the Israelites would worship only him. His claim that he was the only Supreme Being has stunted the spiritual growth of much of humanity for thousands of years. That stunted spiritual growth remains today. The pretender gods programmed us well.

Resistance, Disobedience, and Heroism

If we rebelled, we were beaten down. Horrifying acts of violence were inflicted upon us. The *Old Testament* records Jehovah's killing of 14,000 people at one time (see Numbers 16: 43-49). This was not the enemy: this was Jehovah's own chosen people. I guess, in his eyes, he didn't choose very well. This is more than the 12,000 "enemies" killed during the battle of Jericho.

What was their crime?

Disobedience. Thanks to the religious conditioning begun thousands of years ago, a majority of people – should they ever discover this obscure passage – will simply conclude that they had it coming. After all, they did disobey, didn't they? And Jehovah was God. And he told them not to disobey. God in his wisdom knew what He was doing... didn't he?

However, in a testament to ancient humanity's passion for spiritual freedom, the ancient humans did rebel. Not a few here and there as experienced today, but thousands – perhaps even hundreds of thousands. Sacred books like the *Old Testament* tell of whole cities that chose to be slaughtered rather than submit to the religious conditioning and beliefs of their conquerors.

How come we don't see these bold souls as heroes?

According to Swiss psychologist Carl Gustav Jung, this horror still resides deeply in our collective unconscious. This deep seeded archetype enabled the Spanish Inquisition and the Crusades (along with religious "reformers" like John Calvin) to justify human slaughter whether in the form of "mighty battles" or slowly burning a man at the stake. Past shock lies deep within each and every one of us.

Some of us continue to go intensely into spiritual denial claiming that if it's part of our religious and spiritual heritage, it must be okay. Today, we appear to be more conditioned to past shock – by its very denial – than those who experienced the past shock. Some valiantly tried to stand up to these horrifying events and even attempted to resist the religious conditioning.

Are these people sinners? Or could they be heroes?

The Israelites – even after that uncalled-for bad treatment and slaughter – continued to fight for their oppressors. However, the introduction of religion was beginning to condition them very well. All they had to do was be told by Jehovah or one of his chosen prophets that the people they were about to slaughter were wicked.

When Conditioning Doesn't Work, Intensify the Conditioning

June 1990 – Iraq is our friend and Saddam Hussein is our ally.

August 1990 – Iraq is an evil country and Saddam Hussein all of a sudden is Adolph Hitler.

Anyone who considers the above two sentences as an endorsement of Saddam Hussein is missing the point. The point is that loyalties change quickly because someone tells us that this is what we should do. Friends can shift to being enemies rather quickly. Make a comparison to Adolph Hitler, and the effect is intensified. Only those who boldly research the archives of journalism are aware that George Bush gave Saddam Hussein permission to invade Iraq. Through Ambassador April Glaspe, Bush claimed that he would have no problem with Saddam Hussein's invasion.

When Congress voted by only 53-47 to send troops to Saudi Arabia, some spin control was necessary. Enter a woman who claims she was a nurse and that she saw Iraqi soldiers taking babies out of their incubators and smashing them against the wall. Not until two years after what has been pathetically referred to as the Gulf War, did we discover that the person making the claim was high up in Kuwait's royal family. These claims were total lies.

But these lies got the job done. These lies helped Americans get over "sickly inhibitions" about war and to jump on the "bomb the hell out of Iraq" bandwagon.

Americans felt really righteous after hearing about Iraqi soldiers throwing babies against the wall. The fact that it never happened was irrelevant. It got the job done. It motivated people sitting on the fence to jump down and "stand on the side of right."

This spin control is an ancient art. It began with the pretender gods in ancient history. They most likely were very good at working reluctant warriors into a battle frenzy. Thousands of years later, members of the Crusades returning from Jerusalem would magically work themselves into the same kind of frenzy as they prepared to attack a village of Christians. This was a village that had fed and sustained them on their march to Jerusalem.

But pity the poor Crusaders. They had run out of infidel Islamic types, yet they still had a taste for blood. Boys will be boys.

Whether in the twelfth century or the beginning of the twenty-first century, the conditioning from past shock lives on in ways far more devastating than most humans are willing to admit.

In that ancient past, the newly conditioned humans could have run free – and that's what some of them did. They could have rebelled, and that also is what many did. However, they were always seen as ones that had surrendered to the "forces of darkness."

The pretender gods' conditioning became a sickness. Friend betrayed friend to achieve "spiritual favors" or store up points for the life beyond. As prayers went unanswered, the ante intensified with brutal human sacrifice. Tearing the heart out of a living being "insured" that the crops would grow. Throwing a virgin into a pack of wild animals would soothe the now-departed wrathful gods. Working an extra ten hours a week in the mines would appease the petty pretenders. The priests had it good: all they had to do was make a little trek to the mountain and channel down some good old-fashioned manipulation.

That manipulation continues today.

CHAPTER NINE

The Impact of Modern
Religion on the Human Soul

Many previously mentioned modern authors have claimed that the pretender gods were an extraterrestrial species (Zecharia Sitchin, Neil Freer, William Bramley, etc.) While this is a fairly difficult thesis to prove, these authors have made a good case for their thesis, and it is gaining a surprising acceptance. However, whether the pretender gods were an extraterrestrial species, a species from another dimension, or an advanced human species is not the main point of this book. The focal point instead is the recognition of what was done to ancient humanity in the name of God.

Whatever the pretender god species was, the fact that they left the planet or died off has to be one of the greatest blessings to happen to mankind. If they were indeed an extraterrestrial species, the best use of the Strategic Defense Initiative (Star Wars) technology would be in preventing these interlopers from coming back.

Whoever these technologically advanced beings were, they did humanity significant harm. According to sacred and mythological writings, most of the pretender gods departed around 800 B.C.E. With some exceptions, that's 2,800 years we've had on this planet without any interlopers telling us that they were God. That is 2,800 years without them making us fight wars for them, treating us as slave labor, and then demanding to be worshipped. However, what has been left behind is what author Neil Freer calls a "godspell" – conditioning by the pretender gods which is as strong today as it was when it was administered thousands of years ago.

In fact, after the departure of the pretender gods, a mad rush ensued as the power-driven of the human species rushed to take the place of these gods. They kept the godspell alive by standing in as representative priest or prophet, continuing the "need" to fight holy wars, setting and maintaining the worship trend, and having us look to them for advice and guidance. The only thing they didn't do was to declare themselves as gods. However, they got just as much mileage by declaring themselves God's representatives.

While it is a different orchestra, the slavery-driven symphony was the same. The notes were carefully orchestrated to keep humanity bound to a god who had long departed.

In *Breaking the Godspell*, Neil Freer claims that this ancient conditioning still has humanity by the throat. The godspell continues to stifle us because we have been genetically engineered and conditioned to use only a small part of our brains and minds. Most parents willingly, some even obsessively, pass on this conditioning to their children.

Thanks to the pretender gods, a significant percentage of humanity still believes that a "spiritually correct" cluster of beliefs is the way to salvation. In my twenty-eight years of being a high school and college teacher, I have watched with sadness as some of my students have been beaten down by the "I-am-nothing-without-God" syndrome. Many express a perverse joy in spiritually beating themselves up. Sadly, so many think that this is what the true God wants. From their paradigm, this is the way to be accepted by God and the community of believers.

The tragedy of such behavior is that it is still being reinforced. People will break into applause when someone mentions that they fell flat on their face because they tried to do it "their way," but when they "turned it over to the Lord," He led the way. Admittedly, there is value in seeking guidance from a higher power. However, some push this mentality to such extremes that self-esteem and self-validation are seen as sinful and counterproductive.

Wars are still fought in the name of God. Increasing numbers of religious people are finally starting to realize that a "nail a commie for Christ" mentality may actually be sick. Others are starting to accept the fact that beating up on someone in the name of God actually has nothing to do with God. The more we look at long-time sacred writings with a clear vision, the more we will begin to understand that someone conned us.

Someone programmed us to be good little warriors for the Lord.

During the Gulf War conflict, the mood in this country was "bash the infidel bastards." Just as Jehovah conditioned Joshua to burn and pillage Jericho, so did George Bush have no problem taking out the lives of what Amnesty International estimates now to be 100,000 to 200,000 innocent civilians. Very few were concerned about the women and children that the "smart bombs" killed (This lack of compassion for the innocent victims of war was something relatively new for an American war). You see, they were Arab infidels. And they believed in Allah, which, according to Bible-believing Americans, is not the spiritually correct God.

However, in this particular "war" our collective conditioning reigned supreme. Instead of getting angry at the horrible mistake of bombing a civilian shelter with a two-ton bomb, many Americans instead became angry with Peter Arnett, the CNN journalist who reported this atrocity.

When Ross Perot demanded during the third presidential debate of 1992 that April Glaspe be questioned about her meeting with Saddam Hussein, the press ignored it and on the following day went into great length to explain that Perot was distressed over his daughter's wedding. The press got great mileage over the fact that Perot was a conspiracy nut. The real issue was never addressed.

The combination of past shock, genetic re-engineering, and the awesome psychological conditioning still reigns supreme today. Deep in our psyches we still have a slave chip which says, "If it's right and it's done in the name of the Lord, it's okay.

A doctor's killing of praying Muslims in a Palestinian mosque in Israel. That's okay. Jehovah would have approved. Jehovah loves blood theater.

Palestinian terrorists blowing up Jewish children on a bus in Israel. That's okay. Allah insisted on it.

Serb soldiers gang-raping Muslim women because they did not see them as human – that's okay. Look at all the carnage created by Muslims in the name of Allah.

Might makes right. Revenge is supreme. Slaughter is holy.

This insanity continues because we haven't yet had the courage to recognize that our religious conditioning is insane. As Neil Freer states, we are so stuck in the godspell that we are incapable of recognizing what we are doing to ourselves.

In America, we commit spiritual rape by telling young minds that there is only one true God, and that the true God is the one which they have been conditioned to believe in. In Sunday school I listened as my Sunday school teachers told me that Jesus was the only way to salvation. I was too young, too unsophisticated to resist. These were the authorities. They had to be telling the truth because they were adults, and my mother and father recognized them as authorities.

When I came into Sunday school in tears because "God" had struck Uzzah dead for trying to prevent the Ark of the Covenant from crashing to the ground, I was told – very firmly – that Uzzah had strict orders not to touch the Ark of the Covenant, and that he disobeyed. My concerns were ignored, and the Sunday school teacher went on with her prepared lesson.

102

I was spiritually raped.

Just as the little girl or boy who is not sophisticated enough to resist a sexually deviant relative's sexual advances, so was I not able to resist the conditioning of my Sunday school and Church. I was much more rabid than most, and became Christ's little Bible banger. At school, I carried the Bible on top of my books, solidly convinced that all but a select few in my high school would burn in hell for eternity. Looking back on those days, I see that I was a spiritual pain in the ass.

But I was conditioned, and the conditioning jelled into a belief system that became very difficult to jettison. In my young adolescence, a perverse neighbor rode that conditioning to even deeper levels of spiritual sickness. At her constant urging, I went to Youth for Christ meetings on Saturday nights, often taking friends with me hoping that they would "get saved" and enable me to put yet another notch in my spiritual gun. On Sunday, I went to church twice – once in the morning and once in the evening. I loved singing those hymns with the church's mighty organ pealing in the background. I had no idea that responsive readings and other parts of the ritual were simply keeping me locked in a resurrected conditioning.

It took me nearly forty years to figure it out ... and discover what an awesome price it was.

What is it exactly that all of us eventually need to figure out? What we must have the courage to face is that what makes us feel good religiously may be doing us great spiritual harm. Poet Yevsgeny Yevtushenko in his poem "Lies" points out this sham.

>Telling lies to the young is wrong.
>Proving to them that lies are true is wrong.
>Telling them that God's in his heaven and
>all's well with the world is wrong.
>The young know what you mean.
>The young are people.
>Tell them the difficulties can't be counted,
>And let them see not only what will be
>But see clarity with the present times.
>Say obstacles exist they must encounter
>Sorrow happens, hardship happens.
>The hell with it.
>Who never knew
>The price of happiness will not be happy.

> Forgive no error you recognize,
> It will repeat itself, increase,
> And afterwards our pupils
> Will not forgive what we forgave.

For the lies that the pretender gods told us in telling us that they were God, shame on them.

For allowing these lies to continue in our collective experience, shame on us.

Jehovah, Enlil, Zeus, Ptah and countless other pretenders to Godhood spiritually raped us. To make something holy out of this heinous act merely continues the insanity. We need to forgive the pretender gods for their spiritual brutality, and we need to forgive ourselves for allowing it to continue in acts of slaughter, rigid belief, and "righteousness out of control."

The woman who sings joyfully about the fact that she is saved and that the "unsaved" will burn in hell is continuing the ancient brainwashing.

Those who imply that others are going to hell because they lack a spiritually correct belief cluster are continuing the conditioning.

The "gung ho" soul who "witnesses for the Lord" does no spiritual favors, but instead deepens the devastating godspell which is high on being "right" and low on love and compassion.

The theologically educated who "lead" their flocks continue the devastating lie that God is angry and will send unbelievers to eternal hell continues the spiritual nightmare.

This is a slap in the face to the true God who is incapable of such nonsense. The claim that God has this wonderful gift to offer but will eternally damn anyone who doesn't accept it is an idea that is both illogical and psychologically damaging.

The majority of us are still highly programmed robots incapable of recognizing how dreadfully conditioned we still are. Many still feel guilty if we don't go to mass. Many still think God really cares whether two people making love are married or not. Many still feel we must pass our religious conditioning down upon our children. Many still respond in archetypal joy as "souls" march down to "accept Jesus as their personal savior," not realizing that this is an archetypal conditioning-button from ancient history which evangelical Christians have learned to tap into.

We will not escape our religious conditioning until we are at least willing to explore the possibility that religious conditioning was actually created to block the unfolding of the human experience. We have got to think more about how the pretender gods blocked the flow of our collective souls. This makes much more sense than surrendering to the "fire insurance" mentality of soul–saving.

I know that some reading this will claim I'm an agent for the devil. I'm not. I'm an agent for truth, and truth is more holy than all the "hosannas," and "glory to Gods" uttered in programmed devotion. The fact that I do not yet have a full grasp of the truth does not make me evil. My passion to know the truth is more holy than any "holy certainty" I had before.

A person who embraces a pre-digested belief system is not holy simply because she carries the "correct" belief baggage. This belief baggage comes from the pretender gods, and it must be opened and explored. Once seen for what it is, other things more holy will fill the vacuum.

The great music like Bach's B Minor Mass and Beethoven's Missa Solemnis (Solemn Mass) is more holy than the false gods that allegedly inspired it. A poem from the heart is more holy than most of what Jehovah uttered. John Hus, in his desire to translate the Bible into Czech, had more of a passion for truth than Jehovah, Enlil, Zeus, Wotan, or any other pretender god.

The bad news is that we have been duped for a long time.

The good news is that we can stop it now.

Our path to the truth begins with looking boldly into the past. The more we look into sacred writings with an open heart, the more we will discover that something is wrong with our present approach to the true God.

The collective forces of organized religion do not want to relinquish their psychological stranglehold on collective humanity. Anyone probing into our sacred historical past will realize that before Jesus, accounts of 16 different crucified and resurrected saviors filled the dank halls of our ancient libraries. Each of these saviors was allegedly crucified and resurrected. All seventeen – including Jesus – promised that they would return... very soon. None of them has yet returned.

From 2,500 to 3,500 years ago comes one of these crucified and resurrected saviors named Mithras. How interesting that he – rather than Jesus – was born on December 25th. He was reputed to have been born of a virgin. Pictures of this Persian god Mithras had him carrying a lamb on his shoulders. The Persian sacred texts refer to Mithras as being "the way, the light, and the truth."

Jesus arose in less than two days. However, the confusion between Jesus and Mithras is worth exploring. It was Mithras who claimed that he would come back "to judge the quick and the dead." Those were Mithras' words. After he died, he was placed in a rock tomb, and three days later Mithras allegedly arose from the dead.

The people who believed in the Persian god Mithras referred to this god as the Good Shepherd. He told his followers that there would be a Day of Judgment and that following the judgment non-believers would perish and that believers would live forever in Paradise. (Paradise is a Persian word.)

If you find this amazing, note what the ancient sacred writings tell of another crucified and resurrected savior named Virishna.

The sacred writings tell us that Virishna was born of a "spotless virgin who never had sex with a man." The father of this virgin birth was alleged to be the Holy Spirit. The king at the time of Virishna's birth threatened to have this child put to death, and to save the child's life, the parents had to flee from the child's land of birth. If this doesn't yet sound familiar, consider this. This ancient king had all children less than two years old put to death. Prophecy foretold of the birth of Virishna. Wise men visited Virishna and gave him gifts of frankincense and myrrh. In his life, Virishna was hailed as the "savior of men." In his life he performed miracles of healing, cast out devils, and raised the dead. Not only was Virishna crucified, but he was also crucified between two thieves. Right after his death he descended into hell and then rose from the dead and ascended back to heaven "in the sight of all men."

Both Mithras and Virishna were worshipped as gods 1,500 to 3,500 years before the birth of Jesus.

Folks, we have been conned – first by the pretender gods, then by the ruling priest class which carries on their awesome conditioning early into the twenty-first century. Ignorance still remains a powerful force.

Historically, the apostle Paul was known to be deeply into the Mithras cult. When he allegedly encountered Jesus on the road to Damascus, some scholars claim that he thought that he was encountering the returned Mithras. This may explain why we celebrate Christmas on December 25th instead sometime in April (the month that Jesus was most likely born).

In a very thoroughly researched book, *The Jesus Conspiracy: The Turin Shroud and the Truth about the Resurrection*, German authors Holger Kersten and Elmar R. Gruber tell how the claim that the shroud was a hoax... was actually a hoax in itself. Evidently, as testing was about to get underway, people high up in the Vatican realized that the high amount of blood on the shroud would prove that Jesus was still alive when the shroud was placed on top of him. Fearing what this would do to the Christian faith, people high up in the Vatican realized that such a discovery would damage the belief that Jesus actually was dead and resurrected. Thus, according to Kersten and Gruber, the decision was made to provide four separate pieces of cloth from the fourteenth century.

If this and other aforementioned areas are true, someone wants to keep us in the dark. Some forces high up want humanity kept in the dark. This ruling priest class likes the idea of preaching obedience and submission, despite how inappropriate they are today. The battle cry is no longer "You shall know the truth and the truth will set you free." The battle cry of far too many organized religions appears to be "We will tell you what the truth is, and we don't want you free."

The pretender gods have long departed, but their melody lingers on in devastating harmony. Bach's magnificent *B Minor Mass* begins:

> Kyrie, elision
> [Lord, forgive us]
> Christe, elision
> [Christ, forgive us]
> Kyrie, elision
> [Lord, forgive us]

The true God realizes that we never sinned. He, She or It is not interested in a final judgment where we all experience a terrifying accounting of our sins. *A Course in Miracles* has the following to say about the final judgment:

> God will finally reveal to you that
> you never sinned.

However, I must confess that in my adolescent years I found a perverse joy in being a sin-bound creature, hopelessly hell-bound by his own devices. Being a spiritual cripple gained me great favor in the minions of the spiritual Mafia. To me, God was more a dominatrix inflicting joyous pain upon my limited awareness. My three times reading of the Bible reinforced that if I spiritually screwed up or dared to disobey the divine dictum, mighty Jehovah would bring sickness and anguish into my already convoluted life. Adolescence was bad enough without wondering whether Jehovah was going to give me a cosmic thumping.

The first time I masturbated – which was disgustingly late in my adolescence – I was sure that lighting was going to strike, most likely the offending area of pleasure. My spiritual ass was going to be roasted for sure. I was sure that Mom and Dad knew. And I – the budding theologian,

God's little pain in the ass – was saying to myself: "How can something that feels so good be so sinful?"

I guess you can grasp some idea of my increased spiritual anguish when I finally porked Polly Benson at summer camp. Scenes from the movie *Green Dolphin Street*, where the Earth opened up to swallow screaming humans, swam vividly through my brain.

I am aware that few suffered the spiritual guilt that I did. However, some have it buried so deeply that they are not yet aware of it. I saw this come to the fore in seminary when I looked out the window to behold two cats joyously copulating on the lawn. We shared the house we lived in with another seminary couple. Before I can even assimilate the scene, out runs Mary Lou screaming, "You filthy little kitties!" And, by God, she was going to break it up. At least she didn't condemn the poor kitty to hell. Damn good thing kitties don't have souls.

Amidst all this irreverence and spiritually perverse humor lies a reality that we as humans need to face. We need to get free of the pretender gods' conditioning so that we can begin to experience the true God. I firmly believe that this is the role of the Holy Spirit. The Holy Spirit does not want us to get saved, join a church, give up the joyful aspects of our lives, or read a chapter of the Bible every night. The Holy Spirit wants us to experience joy and fulfillment. That means that those who tap into the guidance of the Holy Spirit just might be led away from their church of fifteen years – and, Jehovah forbid – led away from the well-meant conditioning of our parents. The Holy Spirit speaks through our souls.

I apologize to those humanists, agnostics, and atheists who might be offended by such terminology as "the Holy Spirit" – or even suggesting that the soul is an instrument of God. I do not see atheism as an end product; however, it might be a good way-station as one gets over Christian and Jewish guilt, or any dogma bound to an oppressive religion. I believe that the true God can handle people who insist that society's programmed idea of a God is absurd. I think I can manage to offend just about everyone when I claim that the Holy Spirit might lead a person to Buddhism, Taoism, or even the ideas of the missing militant atheist Madeline Murray O'Hare as a part of their spiritual quest.

While most religious people cannot handle atheism, God evidently can. One of my most joyous moments from Thoreau's *Walden* is Thoreau's pronouncement that the only people that God really feels comfortable with are atheists. While the pretender gods would have snorted with indignation at such a statement, the true God more than likely had a good laugh.

Beliefs do not nurture the experience of God. One becomes a belief collector. This probably happened back in the good ol' days when the emerging humans realized that Jehovah wasn't the only big honcho. Ol' Ba'al was off in the other county doing his pretender god thing. According to some ancient writings, Ba'al had more love and compassion for his followers than Jehovah. Yet, Jehovah made it very clear that any Ba'al-talk was not kosher.

Jehovah backed this up with a cute little stunt when the Ba'al priests chanted for Ba'al to cook the sacrificial meat, and they failed. When the Jehovah groupies did their chanting, fire came down from heaven, and this sure did a lot to help people get back on the Jehovah track. (It wouldn't surprise me to find some document which reveals how Jehovah made a deal with Ba'al to look bad in Israel as long as Jehovah would look bad in Babylon.) The only really good thing I can sense that came out of all of this was the musical rendition of this event in Mendelssohn's oratorio *Elijah*. That scene still gives me goose bumps.

The pretender gods' conditioning demanded rigid and loyal belief. After the pretender gods' departure, the remaining ruling priest class demanded more belief about God. In so doing, they contributed to blocking the actual experience of God.

Organized religion continues this passion for belief and robs us of a passion for God. God does not watch our every move. God is instead a part of us who has given us a soul which can soar above stumbling – without the help of religion, thank you! The true God will not demand that you believe, but the true God did give us the tools to experience. Some churches make a magnificent effort to encourage this, but others are still too locked in dogma and belief to nourish spiritual experience and liberation.

As Columbus moved from terra cognita to terra incognita, the potential for danger was greater. However, despite his unfortunate excesses after "discovering" America, Columbus had the passion of an explorer during that first voyage of discovery.

I urge you who are willing to explore the pretender gods' conditioning to consider the costs of such a voyage.

Very few will cheer for you.

Many will pray for you.

You will have precious few people who understand what you are experiencing. You will have moments of fear, but the philosopher Soren Kirkegaard claimed that "Anxiety is the dizziness of freedom."

My purpose for this book has been to nudge a few thousand people closer to their own spiritual freedom. I have no churches for you to join – and certainly no new religion to explore. Only if I get possessed with the obsession to become exceedingly rich will I ever create a religion. I have no great revealing "must read" books to suggest. Your own soul is a better guide for leading you to any paradigm expanding books.

What if I'm wrong? What if all that this book does is lead people from the True Path? If that's the case, I've figure that Shakespeare, Dante, George Bernard Shaw, Betrand Russell, and my hero – arch-heretic Robert Ingersoll – are all in hell anyway. The prospect of spending eternity with only those who have been "saved" is a consummation devoutly to be unwished.

Through reading this book, you can probably sense that I have a passionate love for music and poetry. I actually get paid for teaching humanities at the college level. This is a nice life. George Friedrich Handel, my favorite composer, wrote religious and secular oratorios. My favorite is *Alexander's Feast*, based on the John Dryden poem of the same name. It tells how the singing poet Timotheus brought down Alexander the Great simply by singing about Alexander's exploits. With this gentle singing accompanying powerful words, Alexander had to face up to his life. I end with the Dryden/Handel words in which the chorus urges Timotheus the poet to wake Alexander up from his drunken sleep.

Break his bonds of sleep asunder.

Rouse him like a peal of thunder.

This is the battle cry of those who will move from the sleep of pretender god conditioning to the path of spiritual liberation.

AFTERWORD

Cracks in the Wall of Illusion

A wall of illusion has been built between humanity and the truth. While the hiding of this truth creates a certain comfort, this comfort is devastating in that it hides realities that have the potential of empowering humans and eventually setting them free.

Comfort has always been a high priority for humans. However, some etymological background is needed to understand fully what comfort actually means. The word is taken from two Latin words: "cum" and "forte." Most with some knowledge of Latin know that these words together mean "with power." Thus, comfort originally meant "to be with power."

When Jesus, referring to the Holy Spirit, promised that he would send the Comforter, he was not promising his disciples some Valium force which would bring relaxation and rest. Instead, Jesus was referring to a force that would empower people. This empowerment must have been in his mind when he stated, "You shall know the truth, and the truth will set you free."

How ironic that the word comfort has been twisted into something which creates "comfort" because it does not deviate from some highly limited paradigm.

How ironic that the maintaining of a paradigm of a religion based on war, slaughter, and captivity has for eons been much more important than going beyond this extremely limited paradigm and searching for a more empowering and life-affirming paradigm.

How ironic that we have a major religion based on the teachings of one who claimed the truth would set people free. Yet, in one of the strangest ironies, this religion must rely on ancient and modern lies in order to survive.

The truth that could set people free is hidden behind a wall.

That wall that hides the truth from people is more revered than the truth itself.

That's the bad news. The good news is that cracks are beginning to appear in this wall of illusion.

111

What people had been willing to accept as the truth, people in increasing numbers are now beginning to question. What is creating this is the acceleration of the information age. Information that is illuminating, embarrassing, and liberating is beginning to force itself into people's consciousness. Those who do not want to face the truth about their horrific past find that a greater effort is required to hold back the forces of truth.

In the 1960's Erik von Daniken came out with a series of ancient astronaut books beginning with *Chariots of the Gods?* Few people noticed the question mark at the end of the title. That book was an exploration. Despite von Daniken's tendency to see an astronaut or spaceman in far too many stone carvings, this book and others which followed blazed a trail of exploration to the idea that thousands of years ago humans may not have been the most intelligent species on the planet. Von Daniken created one of the first cracks in the wall, but despite brisk sales with his books, only a small percentage of people took him seriously.

During this period another scholar was doing intense in-depth research into ancient Sumerian, Assyrian, and Babylonian writings. In what would turn out to be *The Twelfth Planet* in 1976, Zecharia Sitchin was the opposite of von Daniken. He would not write about something unless he had incontrovertible proof about what he was writing. Thus, his books did what von Daniken's failed to do. Sitchin's books attracted the interest of scholars and readers who insist that their reading be supported by scholarly research.

Unlike *Chariots of the Gods?* Sitchin's *The Twelfth Planet* was not an instant seller. While it is one of the most exciting books I have read, it is not an easy book to read. It is filled with historical detail and scholastic support for each of his theories. Yet, I would not have ventured into the theory about the Tower of Babel's being a spaceship launching pad if it had not been for the excellent scholarship of Zecharia Sitchin. His research and related etymology gave this theory enough of a ring of truth to take seriously.

By the 1980's more cracks were beginning to appear in the wall of illusion. Follow-ups to *The Twelfth Planet* were appearing. *Sitchin's The Stairway to Heaven, War of Gods and Men*, and *The Lost Realms* not only appeared in bookstores but also began selling decently enough to keep Sitchin working on what he calls his *Earth Chronicles* series.

Other cracks in the wall also began appearing. One of the main ones was William Bramley's *The Gods of Eden*. Under the aegis of Dahlen Family Press, Bramley printed around 700 copies and felt that he would be lucky if half of those sold. This San Jose lawyer had spent ten years researching war. He noticed that with wars often came UFO activity. As he delved into the ancient history of war, he not only noticed UFO activity but also allegedly superior beings that inhabited those UFOs and actually appeared to influence some of the wars. What I have referred to in this book as pretender gods, Bramley refers to as the custodial gods.

I honestly thought in the late 1980's that his book didn't have a chance. The thesis that the custodial gods were not true gods was controversial enough. However, the equating of these gods to cosmic scum who were exploiting us was strong enough that I thought that would limit his readership. In one harrowing chapter, Bramley states that the Black Plague was a thinning out of the population by the hand of the custodial gods.

His claim that the pictures of death with a scythe were actually pictures of the custodial gods spraying the grain fields with a poison which eventually killed the populations of whole towns. During this plague, UFO activity and the abduction of both humans and cattle were at an all-time high. While my two paragraph description of this Bramley chapter may not sound very credible, the material in his entire chapter is much more believable because of his use of many documents from that period.

I finally met William Bramley at a conference in Los Angeles. It was now the early 1990's, and cracks in the wall were appearing with greater frequency. I had always known that William Bramley was a pseudonym. However, I did not realize what a wise move that was until I talked personally with Bramley. After being picked up by Avon Publishers, his book was now selling in the hundreds of thousands. His law practice was being threatened. Somehow investigators were able to link Bramley with his real name (which I will not divulge).

Something that I didn't think had a chance of selling now was – and still is – a best seller. One cannot go to a large bookstore without seeing at least one copy of *The Gods of Eden*. Bramley's book and the books of Sitchin – as well as others written on the same theme – have paved the way for *Past Shock*.

In addition, Neil Freer's *Breaking the Godspell* was also making a sizable dent. I have referred to this groundbreaking book in this book. A book that would not have had a chance in the 60's and 70's was holding its own through the 80's and 90's. During the first eleven years of his book, Neil has appeared on more than a 100 radio shows. Then in 1998 he came out with *God Games*, which explores in even greater depth the negative impact of ancient religion on modern life and humanity's evolutionary path into the future. This is a solidly researched book which will significantly impact the "godspell" paradigm.

The Shattering 1990's

If little cracks in the wall were seen here and there in the period up through the 1980's, the cracks began appearing with a wonderfully alarming frequency in the 1990's.

The success of the Fox television series *The X Files* opened the way for people to think about realities outside of their own paradigms. The increasing popularity of radio talk shows like *The Art Bell Show* and *The Laura Lee Show* gave a voice to people whose research took them far beyond the realms of a cultural paradigm.

These cracks were not just related to UFOs and ancient astronauts. Researchers like Graham Hancock, Robert Buvall, and John Anthony West were given a platform to speak about the Sphinx and the pyramids which went far beyond what most had learned in school about these amazing structures. Mayan researcher Maurice Cotterel was given a platform at conferences to explain a greater – and more mind expanding – depth about the Mayan structures. Books like Christopher Knight and Robert Lomas' *The Hiram Key* brought a whole new light on what might have happened after the death of Jesus. The idea that Jesus might have survived his ordeal on the cross was no longer considered as heretical as before.

In the true sense of the word, "heresy" people were more willing to choose areas outside of the school, church, and society paradigms.

Religious conspiracy speakers like Jordan Maxwell and David Icke all of a sudden found themselves in great demand. I met Jordan in one of the most delightful of synchronisties. Paul Tice, author of *Triumph of the Human* Spirit and one of the publishers of this book, and I were at the Alexandria II bookstore in Pasadena. With great joy we discovered that Zecharia Sitchin's latest book, *Genesis Revisited,* was finally out. We are standing line, and behind us two other men are getting ready to purchase the same book. What followed was an hour and a half conversation with Leonard and Jordan Maxwell. (There was a brotherhood of people who were reading Sitchin before he became fashionable.)

In the early 1990's, a few people would show up for Jordan's lectures. These were the new paradigm pioneers who were hungry for Jordan's research into why religions were really created. I saw in these increasing numbers of people searchers who wanted to know the truth. These curious people were no longer willing to buy the illusions which their cultures and sub-cultures were perpetuating.

By the mid-1990's Jordan was speaking to sold-out crowds. After finishing a lecture, he would miss a dinner with me because people wanted to talk for hours after he completed a lecture. Often I saw him kicked out of a room because another speaker was scheduled to speak. Yet Jordan and a crowd of thirty to fifty people would continue discussing his material out in the hall or in the lobby of hotel.

That hunger to know has increased to a voracious level. Like the ravens of Indian lore whose voracious appetites increased, so is the collective appetite of people to know the truth.

As stated in the beginning *of The X Files*: "The truth is out there."

With the 1998 release of the *X Files* movie, the audience for the conspiracy oriented *X Files* has significantly increased. The hunger to know not only what is happening now, but what really happened in our ancient past, is increasing at an exponential rate.

It was during the 1990's that my literature students began asking me whether the gods of mythology could have been real historical entities. Only in the 1990's did students begin coming into my office and asking if space beings thousands of years ego created the human race as a race of slaves. Only in the 1990's did I see that many of my conservative Christian students were beginning to be genuinely threatened by some of the things that I brought up in my class.

One of my closest friends and Language Arts Department colleague, Tony Presser, was politely amused by some of the research I was doing about our ancient past. He was the only one in the school that I felt I could trust talking about this material. He thought that names like Enki, Enlil, and Ninhursag were cute to the point of humor. He joyfully, but never offensively, kidded me about these names and what they represented.

Then he read *The Twelfth Planet.*

There, solid research stared him right in his professorial face. His change of behavior reflected that of the newly converted.

I had a class following his in a room where he had just taught. On the board were names like Enki and Enlil and the term "E.Din" which is a Sumerian term from the *Atra Hasis* and the *Enuma Elish* for the place where humans were created. Also on the board from the same sources was the Sumerian term "A.Dam" which is the term the pretender gods used to name their newly created race of humans.

In all of my years as a college teacher, I have never been able to bring myself to talk about my own research other than in the context of mythology. Thus, I asked Tony how talking about this material went over with his students.

"They ate it up. I couldn't believe it," Tony said.

In the fall of 1995, I finally got the courage to do a one-day unit on Sumerian mythology in my world literature class. At least my intention was to keep it to one day. However, some of the more politically correct Greek mythology got sacrificed because of my students' desire to plunge more deeply into the idea that the human race's creation was actually a creation of a slave race. Most of my students were at least willing to explore that advanced beings might be something more than myth.

The fact that someone other than God may have allowed a flood to happen and was watching the mass drowning from above was particularly upsetting for many students. I pointed out the irony that they were strangely more comfortable with an angry god who wiped out all but seven of his creations. What they found hard to take was that some of the pretender gods were weeping as they observed their creations frantically and fearfully attempting to avoid drowning. Even the fact that Enlil felt some remorse while watching was human enough to generate discussion.

Students would secretly make their way to my office to discuss this further. They made sure that no one else was in the office before they would open a discussion in this area. They would become irritated when a student would come in with a rewritten composition and want help with it. (Well, that was what I was paid to do.) The hunger was there. Such a hunger at this or any other college in the 1970's or 1980's would have been extremely rare.

However, as the cracks in the wall of illusion widen, some are able to see through to the other side. While the majority of people are still frightened with what they see, a significantly increasing plurality is hungry enough to walk closer and peek through the cracks. What these bold explorers see both thrills and frightens them. Ancient feelings that they had suppressed for years were now coming to the surface.

Revolutionary Material Creeping into Consensus Reality

Zecharia Sitchin is a devout Jew, and yet he writes about how extraterrestrials created the human race. Graham Hancock is a respected historical scholar. Yet his book *Fingerprints of the Gods* suggests that a group of entities far more intelligent than humans built the Sphinx and the Giza pyramids. Hancock differs from Sitchin: he does not believe that these "gods" were extraterrestrial. Maurice Cotterel in *Supergods* dares to suggest that humans did not build the Mayan and Inca structures. They were built by entities with a far greater intelligence than humans.

These are not new ideas. Many authors were exploring this theme boldly during the early nineteenth century. This was a time when freethinkers and researchers alike were attempting to tell people that organized religion was destroying their very souls. Lecturers like Robert Ingersoll spoke almost nightly to sold out lecture halls pointing out the fallacies and the harm of organized religion.

I knew a mighty big crack had appeared in the wall when a student in one of my critical thinking classes wrote a paper about Robert Ingersoll. When I told him that I had two books of his lectures, he gave me one of those looks that said, "I'm no longer alone." He borrowed both books and devoured their revolutionary ideas. Until our conversation, he had only read about Robert Ingersoll.

North of San Diego is an organization called Truth Seeker. While this organization has been in operation for a long time, it has lately experienced a renaissance. Both Bonnie Lange and Jon Rappoport are dedicated to scooping out "the truth that is out there" and making it available to the average person.

While the average person still isn't very interested in the truth, his or her level of comfort is being increasingly threatened. Evangelical Christian magazines and newspapers are advertising the books of Zecharia Sitchin and Graham Hancock. I commend these Christians who are willing to expose their conditioned comfort to the truth – or at least the potential of truth. During the summer of 1997, I appeared with Jordan Maxwell and Master Ho on four radio shows dealing with ancient astronauts and religious conspiracy. All four of these shows were heard locally.

During the semester following that summer four people visited me to encourage me to remain firm and not lose heart in what is a very conservative part of California – the San Joachin Valley. Others signed up for my classes and were eventually disappointed because I taught students how to write and think rather than talking about what I have covered in this book.

The Native American community is creating other cracks in the wall of illusion. Most of America's indigenous people have very little problem with what is covered by this. Probably no group of people has been more abused and raped by organized religion than America's Native American population. Their legends go further back than recorded history and include many references to the pretender gods.

Native American spiritual leader Robert Morning Sky takes the pretender god thesis one step further and claims that the pretender gods are still "guiding" us in the world of spirit. In one of the most controversial ideas I have encountered, Morning Sky claims that if we are not careful and diligent, our souls will be captured at the moment of death. This way the spirit-based pretender gods can erase all our memories and send us back into a body again, ignorant of who we were and what we had accomplished.

While this is an extremely controversial and very upsetting concept, the fact that people are at least willing to consider this idea is something that was not even possible twenty years ago. While most people are buying into the "wonderful light at the end of the tunnel" concept, increasing numbers of people are willing to go one step further and say, "Could this possibly be a trick of the light?" Doing this requires going beyond that which is simply comforting and exploring more deeply into what might be true.

(I am in no way endorsing this theory. I simply use it as an example of how cracks are beginning to appear in the wall of illusion. Exploration sometimes leads to dead ends. However, the lack of exploration sometimes allows dead material to be substituted for the truth.)

Robert Morning Sky is not alone in this very upsetting viewpoint. Whitley Streiber discusses this concept in his abduction account in *Communion*. Kyle Griffith in *War in Heaven* devotes an entire book to the idea that souls are captured and made to continue their religious worship in another dimension. People who dare to think that the afterlife may not be heaven are harshly treated. Strieber was allegedly told this during an alleged alien abduction. To make sure that Strieber got the point, his soul was separated from his body and imprisoned in a container for what Strieber considered to be a long, long time. He claimed that this was the most terrifying moment of his life.

Whitley Streiber attempted to lecture on his books during the late 1980's. A couple of lectures I attended revealed Whitley to be highly frustrated as a lecturer. I observed him hitting what must have been his nadir when someone told him that he could prevent being abducted by surrounding himself with the white light. Whitley's face became very red, and he couldn't even respond. When the lecture was over, he darted quickly from the podium and disappeared.

Shortly after that lecture, he made a public announcement that he was removing himself from the UFO community.

However, Whitley is back. While the UFO community continues to approach collective insanity, Whitley Strieber has found that people are much more open to what he says. Those new age conventions that he aggressively avoided, he is now warmly embracing. Increasing numbers of people claim to have had experiences like Whitley's.

Even the highly controversial idea of the soul's being captured at the moment of death does not receive the same hostility. The cracks in the wall of illusion are opening wide enough for people to entertain the idea that someone or something on "the other side" doesn't have our best interests in mind.

As many of my Native American friends claim: "The pretender gods didn't really leave; they just moved to another dimension."

Getting Close Enough to Look through the Cracks

From the 1950's through the 1980's, most people who "believed in UFOs" felt that these alleged extraterrestrial beings were our allies and were going to help us get through hard times. Yes, the Hollywood movies portrayed these extraterrestrials as hostile and ready to take over the world. However, the people in the UFO communities of the 1950's and 1960's did not believe this. Those who claimed to be contactees of extraterrestrials said that the extraterrestrials were benign and were going to save us from ourselves.

However, those doing the best research on UFOs are beginning to realize that some form of trickster is generating UFO phenomena. Michael Lindemann and Linda Howe are two of the best UFO researchers on the planet. Both have researched their subjects so well that they are genuinely overwhelmed with whatever is creating UFOs and alien abductions.

During a long dinner session I had with Linda Howe, she often mentioned how frightened she was of what she was discovering. Looking through the cracks of illusion is rarely comforting. Linda has and is still researching the relatively quick disappearance of 1,700 cattle from a New Mexico ranch. If this is a trickster, it is a gruesome trickster who is creating economic havoc.

Another horrifying story comes from an unverifiable source who was researching four California girls. The girls allegedly claimed that they were raped by seven to eight foot reptilian aliens. Two of the girls had their vaginas so badly torn that they had to be hospitalized. Yet one of the girls' accounts has its own unique brand of horror.

Being a devout Christian, this young girl cried out for Jesus to help her. She recollects that Jesus appeared to her, *but did not help her*. Whether this is made up in the mind or actually happened is not the issue as much as the fact that this is what this young lady perceived as happening, and it really rattled her.

The fact that people would even come forward with tales like this is encouraging – even though what's allegedly happening at increasing levels isn't. It indicates that people are more willing to face the darker parts of themselves and their history.

A Rock Song's View of the Tower of Babel – Yet Another Crack

The building of the Tower of Babel was the noble act. The tearing down of the Tower of Babel was the act of a group of pretender gods who became frightened with humanity's increasing mental powers. The scat-

The building of the Tower of Babel was the result of man's effort to reach the heavens.

tering of all these people and confusing their tongues was an act so low that the hordes of Satan, Lucifer, and the Devil simply could not match it. With this act alone, the pretender gods proved that *they* were collectively Satan.

A wonderful crack relating to the Tower of Babel comes from a rock song called "Skyscraper." The song details the joy of potential that the builders were experiencing. They were not arrogant. They were thrilled with what they could accomplish.

The song opens with a command to build bricks for a tower for the world. In this tower all of humanity can "reach anything we suppose, any thing at all." Despite coming from the realm of alternative rock, the beginning of this song is optimistic and expresses both the altruism and the hope of the builders.

The second verse of this song is more revealing and aligned with the ideas of Zecharia Sitchin. The narrator claims that he knows "why you tore it down that day." The song goes on to explain how "God" feared that "He" would get caught, and his people would escape. Thus, "Like a spoiled little baby who can't come out and play, you got your revenge."

In the chorus of "Skyscraper" the humans are speaking to the Destroyer and saying, "Build us up, tear us down, like a skyscraper. Build me up, then tear down these joining walls." The song seems to ask what other than an insane being would tear people down and scatter them all over the earth? This song is a magnificent crack in the world of illusion.

The group that wrote it calls itself Bad Religion.

The Discovery of the Slave Chip – The Biggest Crack

Those who are brave enough to walk up to the wall of illusion and peer through the cracks will discover something not too pleasant. It was unpleasant enough for me to discover that humans were created as a slave race. However, what created initial despair eventually moved me into exhilaration.

During the mid-1980's I had been interviewing hundreds of people for my 1988 book *Knowing When to Quit*. I was coming up against a wall myself. I was exasperated because I was having a hard time finding people who were so fulfilled in their work that their work barely required effort. Yet it was very easy to find people who felt trapped by their jobs and saw no way out. (That was the intent of *Knowing When to Quit* – to show a potential way out.)

I found that these "trapped" people wanted to talk and talk and talk about how trapped they were. But very few wanted to explore ways to move out of their predicaments. If they could just unload about how miserable they were, somehow they would find the strength to go on in a job that they hated. If they felt better, they often left the people they unloaded on feeling depleted.

With trained therapists I had discussed ways to make a bad situation better. With them I researched ways to move beyond a bad situation if no light appeared to be at the end of the tunnel. Yet the interest just wasn't there. If I would suggest some way to move or suggest talking to someone more trained than I was, the majority would quickly move into another story about how their job or spouse abused them.

"What do you think you can do to make this situation better?" I would ask. What I often got in return was strange looks.

Then I had one of the most life-changing experiences of my life. Being interested in *The Epic of Gilgamesh*, I bought a book that promised to shed new light on that epic and provide newly discovered fragments of the epic poem. The book was Zecharia Sitchin's *The Stairway to Heaven.*

I was fascinated with Sitchin's thesis that *The Epic of Gilgamesh* was not myth or fiction but actual history. Sitchin explained that the Gods Enki (Ea), Enlil, and Innana were real beings and that all of these gods came from a planet called Nibiru. I found this fascinating and was enjoying the book. Then my eyes fell on a passage that both rocked me and brought instant clarification:

> Because the Anunnaki [the so-called gods of Sumerian mythology] were close to revolt, they made a decision to create a race of slaves that would do the difficult work in the mines.

This slave race turned out to be the human race.

This was a mighty epiphany. Almost instantly I gained an understanding of the people I was interviewing. A conditioning that made quitting the most horrible marriage or the most devastating job nearly impossible possessed them. This wasn't simply a conditioning in this lifetime. This was an ancient conditioning, and it began with the pretender gods.

The discovery of the slave chip is something very personal. It can only happen within each individual person. The halls of academia aren't going to touch this one. Yet an amazing paradox exists. Those who will boldly explore their conditioned slavery have the best chance of moving from a shallow virtual freedom to a more real freedom of the soul.

The Prison of Virtual Freedom

One of the best films to deal with the slavery that we impose upon ourselves is the 1998 film *Dangerous Beauty*. Its main character is a woman who from her early years is a gifted poet. However, she lives in Venice in 1593 – a society which, despite experiencing the freedom of the Italian Renaissance, would allow women to read, write and study literature only if they went through a rigorous program of learning to pleasure men and learning the arts. (Evidently, knowing the arts was demanded by the men who wanted the services of these highly priced prostitutes.) These high class prostitutes were euphemistically referred to as courtesans. Thus, for Veronica Franco, the real life poet of the film, the only way she could study and write poetry was to become a courtesan.

Thus, to educate herself and develop her poetic soul, she must train to submit herself to men's sexual desires and eventually give herself to the whims of men. Maintaining her sexual purity, and her dignity, will only relegate her to a life of ignorance and limited possibility.

Her desire to be a poet wins out. A strange logic here: if you will be a whore, you can also be a poet.

What was so strange in this film (and was true for late Sixteenth century Venice) was that she was taken seriously as a poet – as long as she remained a courtesan. Men cheer for her as she engages in poetic duels with respected male poets of the time. However, all of this comes at the price of being subject to the whims of the city's leading fathers.

In a poignant scene between the courtesan and a girlhood friend, the girlhood friend is bitter and jealous. However she is put down quickly with a terse reply:

> We're both in cages.
> I just have a bigger cage.

This brings to mind the quote by Gurdjieff used earlier in this book:

> One cannot escape from prison until he is
> willing to admit that he is indeed in prison.

During these millennial times we have the majority of humans who are so locked into their slave chips that they are simply satisfied to get a larger cell. In the time of past shock, they would have been promoted to the role of foreman in the mines. The work was still brutal, but not as brutal as the grunts mining the ore.

In present times, a bigger cage might mean a higher salary and promotion to a higher prestige position. The person may feel better about his circumstances, but he is still a slave if he is not fulfilled and joyful about his work. He is still locked into a slave ship mentality if the increased prestige and prosperity come at the cost of satisfaction and inner peace.

The cracks in the wall of illusion are causing increasing numbers of people to look at the fruits of this conditioned slave chip.

The majority of people on planet earth are still happy with a bigger cage.

However, bigger cracks are appearing in the wall of illusion. Increasing numbers of people are waking up to the reality that the point of life is to forget about the bigger cage and get out of prison.

INDEX

Triumph of the Human Spirit: The Greatest Achievements of the Human Soul and How Its Power Can Change Your Life, by Paul Tice. A triumph of the human spirit happens when we know we are right about something, put our heart into achieving its goal, and then succeed. There is no better feeling. People throughout history have triumphed while fighting for the highest ideal of all -- spiritual truth. Tice brings you back to relive and explore history's most incredible spiritual moments, bringing you into the lives of visionaries and great leaders who were in touch with their souls and followed their hearts. They explored God in their own way, exposed corruption and false teachings, or freed themselves and others from suppression. People like Gandhi, Joan of Arc, and Dr. King expressed exactly what they believed and changed the entire course of history. They were eliminated through violence, but on a spiritual level achieved victory because of their strong moral cause. Their spirit lives on, and the world was greatly improved. Tice covers other movements and people who may have physically failed, but spiritually triumphed. This book not only documents the history of spiritual giants, it shows how you can achieve your own spiritual triumph. In today's world we are free to explore the truth without fear of being tortured or executed. As a result, the rewards are great. Various exercises will strengthen the soul and reveal its hidden power. One can discover their true spiritual source with this work and will be able to tap into it. This is the perfect book for all those who believe in spiritual freedom and have a passion for the truth. **ISBN 1-885395-57-4 · 295 pages · 6 x 9 · trade paper · illustrated · $19.95**

Mysteries Explored: The Search for Human Origins, UFOs, and Religious Beginnings, **by Jack Barranger and Paul Tice**. Jack Barranger and Paul Tice are two authors who have combined forces in an overall investigation into human origins, religion, mythology, UFOs, and other unexplained phenomena. In the first chapter, "The Legacy of Zecharia Sitchin", Barranger covers the importance of Sitchin's *Earth Chronicles* books, which is creating a revolution in the way we look at our past. In "The First Dragon" chapter, Tice examines the earliest known story containing dragons, coming from Sumerian/Babylonian mythology. In "Past Shock", Barranger suggests that events which happened thousands of years ago very strongly impact humanity today. In "UFOs: From Earth or Outer Space?" Tice explores the evidence for aliens being from other earthly dimensions as opposed to having an extraterrestrial origin. "Is Religion Harmful?" looks at the origins of religion and why the entire idea may no longer be working for us, while "A Call to Heresy" shows how Jesus and the Buddha were considered heretics in their day, and how we have reached a critical point in our present spiritual development that requires another such leap. Aside from these chapters, the book also contains a number of outrageous (but discontinued) newsletters, including: Promethean Fire, Pleiadian Poop, and Intrusions. **ISBN 1-58509-101-4 · 104 pages · 6 x 9 · trade paper · $12.95**

Mushrooms and Mankind: The Impact of Mushrooms on Human Consciousness and Religion, by James Arthur. For thousands of years on our planet, humanity has been involved in a symbiotic relationship with plants. Not only have plants supplied mankind with a never-ending food source, the necessary nourishment for our bodies and life itself, but they have also served us in another way: an extremely important and intricate one, yet an often overlooked one. This book uncovers the natural link between man, consciousness, and God. This discovery may at first seem abstract, wishful thinking, or even impossible; yet as evidence presented on these pages unfolds, you may find that its understanding does not require as much of a leap of faith as you might think. This may be the most significant discovery in the entire field of religious knowledge ever to happen in the history of mankind. Should people use

this knowledge, it will allow many on this planet to put their differences aside, and join in the understanding that each and every one of us may now experience that which has been, until this time, hidden away in the recesses of our spiritual history. We may at last be able to open ourselves to an entirely new and valuable consciousness. **ISBN 1-58509-151-0 · 103 pages · 6 x 9 · trade paper · $12.95**

Of Heaven and Earth: Essays Presented at the First Sitchin Studies Day, edited by Zecharia Sitchin. Zecharia Sitchin's previous books have sold millions around the world. This book, first published in 1996, contains further information on his incredible theories about the origins of mankind and the intervention by intelligences beyond the Earth. Sitchin, in previous works, offers the most scholarly and convincing approach to the ancient astronaut theory you will most certainly ever find. This book offers the complete transcript of the first Sitchin Studies Day, held in Denver, Colorado on Oct. 6, 1996. Zecharia Sitchin's keynote address opens the book, followed by six other prominent speakers whose work has been influenced by Sitchin. The other contributors to the book include two university professors, a clergyman, a UFO expert, a philosopher, and a novelist—who joined Zecharia Sitchin in Denver, Colorado, to describe how his findings and conclusions have affected what they teach and preach. They all seem to agree that the myths of ancient peoples were actual events as opposed to being figments of imaginations. Another point of agreement is in Sitchin's work being the early part of a new paradigm—one that is already beginning to shake the very foundations of religion, archaeology and our society in general. **BT-175 • ISBN 1-885395-17-5 • 164 pages • 5 1/2 x 8 1/2 • trade paper • illustrated • $14.95**

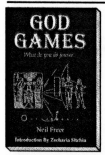

God Games: What Do You Do Forever? by Neil Freer. "Then came Neil Freer [who] undertook a different kind of mind-boggling task. If all that I had concluded was true, he said, what does it all mean, not to the human race and the planet in general—what does it mean to the individuals, to each one of us? He titles his new book *God Games*. But, if all the above is the Truth, it is not a game." Zecharia Sitchin (from the Introduction). This new book by Neil Freer, author of *Breaking the Godspell*, outlines the human evolutionary scenario far into the future. Freer describes what's in store for us as our dawning genetic enlightenment reveals the new human and the racial maturity of a new planetary civilization on the horizon. We all can contribute to our future as we evolve from a slave species to far beyond what we could previously even imagine. The godspell broken, we new humans will create our own realities and play our own "god games." According to Freer, once we understand our true genetic history we will eventually move beyond the gods, religion, linear consciousness and even death. It is quite possible that great thinkers in the future will look back on this book as being the one which opened the door to our full evolutionary potential and a new paradigm. Neil Freer is a brilliant philosopher, focused on the freedom of the individual and what it means to be truly human. This book will make you think in new and different ways. Accept the challenge of *God Games* and you will be greatly rewarded. See page 16 for other products by Neil Freer. **BT-396 • ISBN 1-885395-39-6 • 312 pages • 6 x 9 • trade paper • $19.95**

BREAKING THE GODSPELL: THE POLITICS OF OUR EVOLUTION, by Neil Freer. In *Breaking the Godspell* Neil Freer explores the archaeological, astronomical and genetic evidence for our being a half-alien, genetically engineered species. He presents the mind-boggling ramifications of this new paradigm which correct and resolve the Creationist-Evolutionary conflict, afford a generic definition of human nature, and the potential to rethink the planet. We are about to step out of racial adolescence into stellar society. Zecharia Sitchin, author of *The 12th Planet* writes "It is gratifying that a mere decade after the publication of my work, an author with the grasp that Neil Freer displays in *Breaking the Godspell* has set out to probe what the recognition of the existence and Earth-visits of the Nefilim can mean—not just to scientists and theologians—but to each human being upon this planet Earth." This book is an encyclopedia of innovative ideas and engaging speculation. It will alter your consciousness. It could change your life. BT-361 • ISBN 1-885395-36-1 • 151 pages • 6 x 9 • trade paper • $15.95

FLYING SERPENTS AND DRAGONS: The Story of Mankind's Reptilian Past, By R.A. Boulay. Revised and expanded edition. This highly original work deals a shattering blow to all our preconceived notions about our past and human origins. Worldwide legends refer to giant flying lizards and dragons which came to this planet and founded the ancient civilizations of Mesopotamia, Egypt, India and China. Who were these reptilian creatures? This book provides the answers to many of the riddles of history such as what was the real reason for man's creation, why did Adam lose his chance at immortality in the Garden of Eden, who were the Nefilim who descended from heaven and mated with human women, why the serpent take such a bum rap in history, why didn't Adam and Eve wear clothes in Eden, what were the "crystals" or "stones" that the ancient gods fought over, why did the ancient Sumerians call their major gods USHUMGAL, which means literally "great fiery, flying serpent," what was the role of the gigantic stone platform at Baalbek, and what were the "boats of heaven" in ancient Egypt and the "sky chariots" of the Bible? ISBN 1-885395-38-8 • 276 pages • 6 x 9 • trade paperback • $19.95 •

Space Travelers and the Genesis of the Human Form: Evidence of Intelligent Contact in the Solar System, by Joan d'Arc. Believers in extraterrestrial intelligent life (ETI) have no doubt been confronted with the few standard arguments covered in this book that are pitched by most skeptics. But are they logical and internally consistent? Or are they based on mistaken assumptions, government-media hogwash, and outmoded scientific concepts? Even skeptics may want to explore the logical grounds upon which their staunch protest against the existence of ETI is founded. Can Darwinian evolution actually prove we are alone in the Universe? This book illustrates that Darwinian evolution is actually not an empirically predictable or testable scientific paradigm. Darwinian evolution is a circular argument which serves to keep Earth humans earthbound. This book also shows that ancient artifacts on Mars and the Moon are evidence of "Game Wardens" in our own solar system. Could the Earth be a controlled DNA repository for the ongoing creation and dissemination of life forms, including humans. BT-278 • ISBN 1-58509-127-8 • 208 pages • 6 x 9 • trade paper • illustrated • $18.95

Matrix of Power: How the World has Been Controlled by Powerful People Without Your Knowledge, by Jordan Maxwell. Jordan Maxwell is considered to be the world's foremost authority on ancient religions and modern conspiracies. His work on the true meaning of symbols, logos, and company insignias has also fascinated audiences around the world for years. He grew up in a family that had high-ranking insiders in international politics and religion, so was privy to behind the scenes information that few people could imagine during the time that he was growing up. This intrigued him, and set him off on a lifetime of investigation. This book is the result, or rather a partial result, of his many years of investigation. Who really runs the world? Who controls the money, the politics, and almost every facet

of your life without you knowing a thing about it? Is such a thing possible? Explore this fascinating subject with a man who has devoted a lifetime of study to uncovering our "hidden masters." There are a number of more highly visible researchers who are speaking out and writing on this subject. Jordan Maxwell has, for the most part, remained in the shadows—similar to those who manipulate world affairs. Few people know that the primary source for many of these people has been Jordan Maxwell. His files of documentation are enormous, yet this is his first book as a sole author (he previously appeared in *The Book Your Church Does Not Want You to Read* and *That Old Time Religion,* with Paul Tice). He has made countless radio and TV appearances including three CBS television specials, and has numerous videos of his work available. We are honored to present this powerful and informative book to the public. BT-200 • ISBN 1-58509-120-0 • 103 pages • 6 x 9 • trade paper • $12.95

Of Heaven and Earth: Essays Presented at the First Sitchin Studies Day, edited by Zecharia Sitchin. ISBN 1-885395-17-5 • 164 pages • 5 1/2 x 8 1/2 • trade paper • illustrated • $14.95

God Games: What Do You Do Forever?, by Neil Freer. ISBN 1-885395-39-6 • 312 pages • 6 x 9 • trade paper • $19.95

Breaking the Godspel: The Politics of Our Evolution, by Neil Freer. ISBN 1-885395-36-1 • 151 pages • 6 x 9 • trade paper • $15.95

Past Shock: The Origin of Religion and Its Impact on the Human Soul, by Jack Barranger. ISBN 1-885395-08-6 • 126 pages • 6 x 9 • trade paper • illustrated • $12.95

Triumph of the Human Spirit: The Greatest Achievements of the Human Soul and How Its Power Can Change Your Life, by Paul Tice. ISBN 1-885395-57-4 • 295 pages • 6 x 9 • trade paper • illustrated • $19.95

Space Travelers and the Genesis of the Human Form: Evidence of Intelligent Contact in the Solar System, by Joan d'Arc. ISBN 1-58509-127-8 • 208 pages • 6 x 9 • trade paper • illustrated • $18.95

Phenomenal World:Remote Viewing, Astral Travel, Apparitions, ETs, and Lucid Dreams, by Joan d'Arc. ISBN 1-58509-128-6 • 211 pages • 6 x 9 • trade paper • illustrated • $18.95

Mysteries Explored: The Search for Human Origins, UFOs, and Religious Beginnings, by Jack Barranger and Paul Tice. ISBN 1-58509-101-4 • 104 pages • 6 x 9 • trade paper • $12.95

Mushrooms and Mankind: The Impact of Mushrooms on Human Consciousness and Religion, by James Arthur. ISBN 1-58509-151-0 • 103 pages • 6 x 9 • trade paper • $12.95

Vril or Vital Magnetism, with an Introduction by Paul Tice.ISBN 1-58509-030-1 • 124 pages • 5 1/2 x 8 1/2 • trade paper • $12.95

The Odic Force: Letters on Od and Magnetism, by Karl von Reichenbach. ISBN 1-58509-001-8 • 192 pages • 6 x 9 • trade paper • $15.95

The New Revelation: The Coming of a New Spiritual Paradigm, by Arthur Conan Doyle.ISBN 1-58509-220-7 • 124 pages • 6 x 9 • trade paper • $12.95

The Astral World: Its Scenes, Dwellers, and Phenomena, by Swami Panchadasi. ISBN 1-58509-071-9 • 104 pages • 6 x 9 • trade paper • $11.95

Reason and Belief: The Impact of Scientific Discovery on Religious and Spiritual Faith, by Sir Oliver Lodge. ISBN 1-58509-226-6 • 180 pages • 6 x 9 • trade paper • $17.95

William Blake: A Biography, by Basil De Selincourt. ISBN 1-58509-225-8 • 384 pages • 6 x 9 • trade paper • $28.95

The Divine Pymander: And Other Writings of Hermes Trismegistus, translated by John D. Chambers. ISBN 1-58509-046-8 • 196 pages • 6 x 9 • trade paper • $16.95

Theosophy and The Secret Doctrine, by Harriet L. Henderson. Includes *H.P. Blavatsky: An Outline of Her Life*, by Herbert Whyte, ISBN 1-58509-075-1 • 132 pages • 6 x 9 • trade paper • $13.95

The Light of Egypt, Volume One: The Science of the Soul and the Stars, by Thomas H. Burgoyne. ISBN 1-58509-051-4 • 320 pages • 6 x 9 • trade paper • illustrated • $24.95

The Light of Egypt, Volume Two: The Science of the Soul and the Stars, by Thomas H. Burgoyne. ISBN 1-58509-052-2 • 224 pages • 6 x 9 • trade paper • illustrated • $17.95

The Jumping Frog and 18 Other Stories: 19 Unforgettable Mark Twain Stories, by Mark Twain. ISBN 1-58509-200-2 • 128 pages • 6 x 9 • trade paper • $12.95

The Devil's Dictionary: A Guidebook for Cynics, by Ambrose Bierce. ISBN 1-58509-016-6 • 144 pages • 6 x 9 • trade paper • $12.95

The Smoky God: Or The Voyage to the Inner World, by Willis George Emerson. ISBN 1-58509-067-0 • 184 pages • 6 x 9 • trade paper • illustrated • $15.95

A Short History of the World, by H.G. Wells. ISBN 1-58509-211-8 • 320 pages • 6 x 9 • trade paper • $24.95

The Voyages and Discoveries of the Companions of Columbus, by Washington Irving. ISBN 1-58509-500-1 • 352 pages • 6 x 9 • hard cover • $39.95

History of Baalbek, by Michel Alouf. ISBN 1-58509-063-8 • 196 pages • 5 x 8 • trade paper • illustrated • $15.95*Ancient Egyptian Masonry: The Building Craft*, by Sommers Clarke and R. Engelback.ISBN 1-58509-059-X • 350 pages • 6 x 9 • trade paper • illustrated • $26.95

That Old Time Religion: The Story of Religious Foundations, by Jordan Maxwell and Paul Tice. ISBN 1-58509-100-6 • 103 pages • 6 x 9 • trade paper • $12.95

The Book of Enoch: A Work of Visionary Revelation and Prophecy, Revealing Divine Secrets and Fantastic Information about Creation, Salvation, Heaven and Hell, translated by R. H. Charles. ISBN 1-58509-019-0 • 152 pages • 5 1/2 x 8 1/2 • trade paper • $13.95

The Book of Enoch: Translated from the Editor's Ethiopic Text and Edited with an Enlarged Introduction, Notes and Indexes, Together with a Reprint of the Greek Fragments, edited by R. H. Charles. ISBN 1-58509-080-8 • 448 pages • 6 x 9 • trade paper • $34.95

The Book of the Secrets of Enoch, translated from the Slavonic by W. R. Morfill. Edited, with Introduction and Notes by R. H. Charles. ISBN 1-58509-020-4 • 148 pages • 5 1/2 x 8 1/2 • trade paper • $13.95

Enuma Elish: The Seven Tablets of Creation, Volume One, by L. W. King. ISBN 1-58509-041-7 • 236 pages • 6 x 9 • trade paper • illustrated • $18.95

Enuma Elish: The Seven Tablets of Creation, Volume Two, by L. W. King. ISBN 1-58509-042-5 • 260 pages • 6 x 9 • trade paper • illustrated • $19.95

Enuma Elish, Volumes One and Two: The Seven Tablets of Creation, by L. W. King. Two volumes from above bound as one. ISBN 1-58509-043-3 • 496 pages • 6 x 9 • trade paper • illustrated • $38.90

The Archko Volume: Documents that Claim Proof to the Life, Death, and Resurrection of Christ, by Drs. McIntosh and Twyman. ISBN 1-58509-082-4 • 248 pages • 6 x 9 • trade paper • $20.95

The Lost Language of Symbolism: An Inquiry into the Origin of Certain Letters, Words, Names, Fairy-Tales, Folklore, and Mythologies, by Harold Bayley. ISBN 1-58509-070-0 • 384 pages • 6 x 9 • trade paper • $27.95

The Book of Jasher: A Suppressed Book that was Removed from the Bible, Referred to in Joshua and Second Samuel, translated by Albinus Alcuin (800 AD). ISBN 1-58509-081-6 • 304 pages • 6 x 9 • trade paper • $24.95

The Bible's Most Embarrassing Moments, with an Introduction by Paul Tice. ISBN 1-58509-025-5 • 172 pages • 5 x 8 • trade paper • $14.95

History of the Cross: The Pagan Origin and Idolatrous Adoption and Worship of the Image, by Henry Dana Ward. ISBN 1-58509-056-5 • 104 pages • 6 x 9 • trade paper • illustrated • $11.95

Was Jesus Influenced by Buddhism? A Comparative Study of the Lives and Thoughts of Gautama and Jesus, by Dwight Goddard. ISBN 1-58509-027-1 • 252 pages • 6 x 9 • trade paper • $19.95

History of the Christian Religion to the Year Two Hundred, by Charles B. Waite. ISBN 1-885395-15-9 • 556 pages. • 6 x 9 • hard cover • $25.00

Symbols, Sex, and the Stars, by Ernest Busenbark. ISBN 1-885395-19-1 • 396 pages • 5 1/2 x 8 1/2 • trade paper • $22.95

History of the First Council of Nice: A World's Christian Convention, A.D. 325, by Dean Dudley. ISBN 1-58509-023-9 • 132 pages • 5 1/2 x 8 1/2 • trade paper • $12.95

The World's Sixteen Crucified Saviors, by Kersey Graves. ISBN 1-58509-018-2 • 436 pages • 5 1/2 x 8 1/2 • trade paper • $29.95

Babylonian Influence on the Bible and Popular Beliefs: A Comparative Study of Genesis I.2, by A. Smythe Palmer. ISBN 1-58509-000-X • 124 pages • 6 x 9 • trade paper • $12.95

Biography of Satan: Exposing the Origins of the Devil, by Kersey Graves. ISBN 1-885395-11-6 • 168 pages • 5 1/2 x 8 1/2 • trade paper • $13.95

The Malleus Maleficarum: The Notorious Handbook Once Used to Condemn and Punish "Witches", by Heinrich Kramer and James Sprenger. ISBN 1-58509-098-0 • 332 pages • 6 x 9 • trade paper • $25.95

Crux Ansata: An Indictment of the Roman Catholic Church, by H. G. Wells.ISBN 1-58509-210-X • 160 pages • 6 x 9 • trade paper • $14.95

Emanuel Swedenborg: The Spiritual Columbus, by U.S.E. (William Spear). ISBN 1-58509-096-4 • 208 pages • 6 x 9 • trade paper • $17.95

Dragons and Dragon Lore, by Ernest Ingersoll. ISBN 1-58509-021-2 • 228 pages • 6 x 9 • trade paper • illustrated • $17.95

The Vision of God, by Nicholas of Cusa. ISBN 1-58509-004-2 • 160 pages • 5 x 8 • trade paper • $13.95

The Historical Jesus and the Mythical Christ: Separating Fact From Fiction, by Gerald Massey. ISBN 1-58509-073-5 • 244 pages • 6 x 9 • trade paper • $18.95

Gog and Magog: The Giants in Guildhall; Their Real and Legendary History, with an Account of Other Giants at Home and Abroad, by F.W. Fairholt. ISBN 1-58509-084-0 • 172 pages • 6 x 9 • trade paper • $16.95

The Origin and Evolution of Religion, by Albert Churchward. ISBN 1-58509-078-6 • 504 pages • 6 x 9 • trade paper • $39.95

The Origin of Biblical Traditions, by Albert T. Clay. ISBN 1-58509-065-4 • 220 pages • 5 1/2 x 8 1/2 • trade paper • $17.95

Aryan Sun Myths, by Sarah Elizabeth Titcomb. Introduction by Charles Morris. ISBN 1-58509-069-7 • 192 pages • 6 x 9 • trade paper • $15.95

The Social Record of Christianity, by Joseph McCabe. Includes **The Lies and Fallacies of the Encyclopedia Britannica**, ISBN 1-58509-215-0 • 204 pages • 6 x 9 • trade paper • $17.95

The History of the Christian Religion and Church During the First Three Centuries, by Dr. Augustus Neander. ISBN 1-58509-077-8 • 112 pages • 6 x 9 • trade paper • $12.95

Ancient Symbol Worship: Influence of the Phallic Idea in the Religions of Antiquity, by Hodder M. Westropp and C. Staniland Wake. ISBN 1-58509-048-4 • 120 pages • 6 x 9 • trade paper • illustrated • $12.95

The Gnosis: Or Ancient Wisdom in the Christian Scriptures, by William Kingsland. ISBN 1-58509-047-6 • 232 pages • 6 x 9 • trade paper • $18.95

The Evolution of the Idea of God: An Inquiry into the Origin of Religions, by Grant Allen. ISBN 1-58509-074-3 • 160 pages • 6 x 9 • trade paper • $14.95

Sun Lore of All Ages: A Survey of Solar Mythology, Folklore, Customs, Worship, Festivals, and Superstition, by William Tyler Olcott. ISBN 1-58509-044-1 • 316 pages • 6 x 9 • trade paper • $24.95

Nature Worship: An Account of Phallic Faiths and Practices Ancient and Modern, by the Author of Phallicism with an Introduction by Tedd St. Rain. ISBN 1-58509-049-2 • 112 pages • 6 x 9 • trade paper • illustrated • $12.95

Life and Religion, by Max Muller. ISBN 1-885395-10-8 • 237 pages • 5 1/2 x 8 1/2 • trade paper • $14.95

Jesus: God, Man, or Myth? An Examination of the Evidence, by Herbert Cutner. ISBN 1-58509-072-7 • 304 pages • 6 x 9 • trade paper • $23.95

Pagan and Christian Creeds: Their Origin and Meaning, by Edward Carpenter. ISBN 1-58509-024-7 • 316 pages • 5 1/2 x 8 1/2 • trade paper • $24.95

The Christ Myth: A Study, by Elizabeth Evans. ISBN 1-58509-037-9 • 136 pages • 6 x 9 • trade paper • $13.95

Popery: Foe of the Church and the Republic, by Joseph F. Van Dyke. ISBN 1-58509-058-1 • 336 pages • 6 x 9 • trade paper • illustrated • $25.95

Career of Religious Ideas, by Hudson Tuttle. ISBN 1-58509-066-2 • 172 pages • 5 x 8 • trade paper • $15.95

Buddhist Suttas: Major Scriptural Writings from Early Buddhism, by T.W. Rhys Davids. ISBN 1-58509-079-4 • 376 pages • 6 x 9 • trade paper • $27.95

Early Buddhism, by T. W. Rhys Davids. Includes **Buddhist Ethics: The Way to Salvation?**, by Paul Tice. ISBN 1-58509-076-X • 112 pages • 6 x 9 • trade paper • $12.95

The Fountain-Head of Religion: A Comparative Study of the Principal Religions of the World and a Manifestation of their Common Origin from the Vedas, by Ganga Prasad. ISBN 1-58509-054-9 • 276 pages • 6 x 9 • trade paper • $22.95

India: What Can It Teach Us?, by Max Muller. ISBN 1-58509-064-6 • 284 pages • 5 1/2 x 8 1/2 • trade paper • $22.95

Matrix of Power: How the World has Been Controlled by Powerful People Without Your Knowledge, by Jordan Maxwell. ISBN 1-58509-120-0 • 104 pages • 6 x 9 • trade paper • $12.95

Cyberculture Counterconspiracy: A Steamshovel Web Reader, Volume One, edited by Kenn Thomas. ISBN 1-58509-125-1 • 180 pages • 6 x 9 • trade paper • illustrated • $16.95

Cyberculture Counterconspiracy: A Steamshovel Web Reader, Volume Two, edited by Kenn Thomas. ISBN 1-58509-126-X • 132 pages • 6 x 9 • trade paper • illustrated • $13.95

Oklahoma City Bombing: The Suppressed Truth, by Jon Rappoport. ISBN 1-885395-22-1 • 112 pages • 5 1/2 x 8 1/2 • trade paper • $12.95

Secret Societies and Subversive Movements, by Nesta H. Webster. ISBN 1-58509-092-1 • 432 pages • 6 x 9 • trade paper • $29.95

The Secret Doctrine of the Rosicrucians, by Magus Incognito. ISBN 1-58509-091-3 • 256 pages • 6 x 9 • trade paper • $20.95

The Origin and Evolution of Freemasonry: Connected with the Origin and Evolution of the Human Race, by Albert Churchward. ISBN 1-58509-029-8 • 240 pages • 6 x 9 • trade paper • $18.95

The Lost Key: An Explanation and Application of Masonic Symbols, by Prentiss Tucker. ISBN 1-58509-050-6 • 192 pages • 6 x 9 • trade paper • illustrated • $15.95

The Character, Claims, and Practical Workings of Freemasonry, by Rev. C.G. Finney. ISBN 1-58509-094-8 • 288 pages • 6 x 9 • trade paper • $22.95

The Secret World Government or "The Hidden Hand": The Unrevealed in History, by Maj.-Gen., Count Cherep-Spiridovich. ISBN 1-58509-093-X • 203 pages • 6 x 9 • trade paper • $17.95

The Magus, Book One: A Complete System of Occult Philosophy, by Francis Barrett. ISBN 1-58509-031-X • 200 pages • 6 x 9 • trade paper • illustrated • $16.95

The Magus, Book Two: A Complete System of Occult Philosophy, by Francis Barrett. ISBN 1-58509-032-8 • 220 pages • 6 x 9 • trade paper • illustrated • $17.95

The Magus, Book One and Two: A Complete System of Occult Philosophy, by Francis Barrett. ISBN 1-58509-033-6 • 420 pages • 6 x 9 • trade paper • illustrated • $34.90

The Key of Solomon The King, by S. Liddell MacGregor Mathers. ISBN 1-58509-022-0 • 152 pages • 6 x 9 • trade paper • $22.95

Magic and Mystery in Tibet, by Alexandra David-Neel. ISBN 1-58509-097-2 • 352 pages • 6 x 9 • trade paper • $26.95

The Comte de St. Germain, by I. Cooper Oakley. ISBN 1-58509-068-9 • 280 pages • 6 x 9 • trade paper • illustrated • $22.95

Alchemy Rediscovered and Restored, by A. Cockren. ISBN 1-58509-028-X • 156 pages • 5 1/2 x 8 1/2 • trade paper • $13.95

The 6th and 7th Books of Moses, with an Introduction by Paul Tice. ISBN 1-58509-045-X • 188 pages • 6 x 9 • trade paper • illustrated • $16.95

Printed in the United States
16760LVS00005BA/206